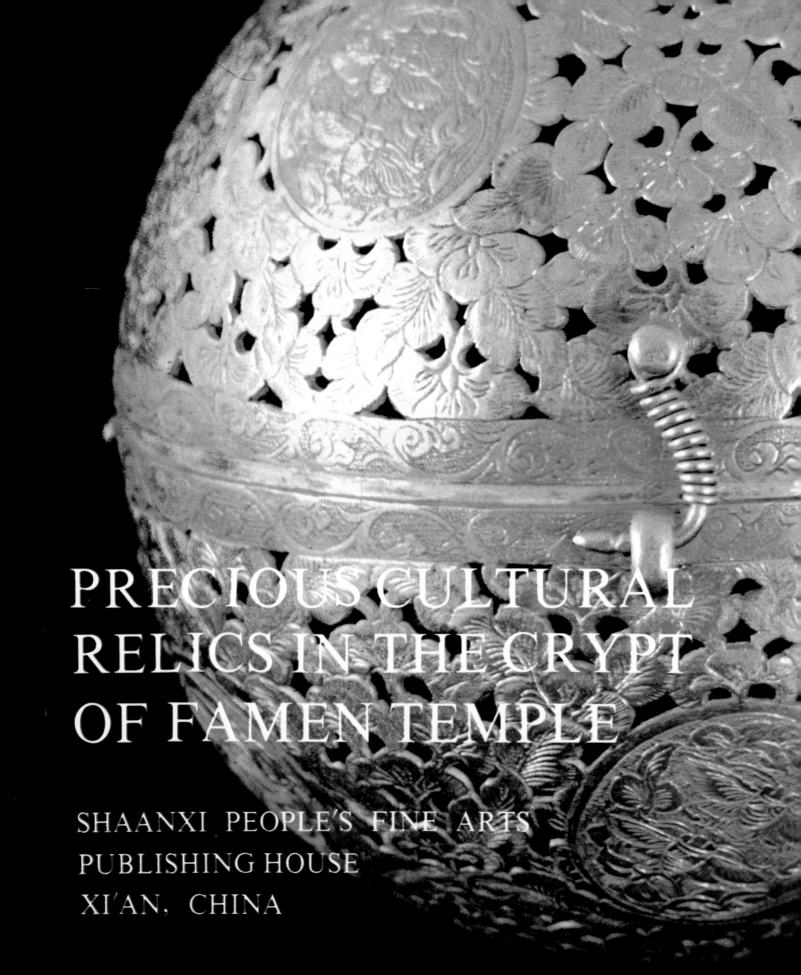

PRECIOUS CULTURAL RELICS IN THE CRYPT OF FAMEN TEMPLE

SHAANXI PEOPLE'S FINE ARTS
PUBLISHING HOUSE
XI'AN, CHINA

法门寺
地宫珍宝

法门寺考古队

石兴邦　编选　　韩　伟　图版解说

陕西人民美術出版社

中国·西安

前　言

石 兴 邦

　　1987 年，我们对法门寺真身宝塔地宫的发掘中，获得了一批极其珍贵的历史文物。这批文物对研究唐代的宗教史、工艺史和社会史方面提供了颇富历史价值的实物史料，引起社会各阶层和学术界各方面人士的极大重视、关心和珍爱。目前，我们正日以继夜地在整理编写研究报告，以期早日公诸于世，以贡献于四化建设。在正式报告未发表之前，为了满足广大群众和学术界同志的迫切需要，我们先选其有代表性的部分文物，编印成册，以飨读者。

　　法门寺，位于扶风县之法门寺乡，南距县城十公里，东南距西安约一百二十公里，是我国境内安置释迦牟尼真身舍利的著名寺院。据传，该寺始建于东汉桓、灵年间（公元147——189 年），素有“关中塔庙之祖”的美称。唐时，该寺颇为隆盛。寺内原有四重木塔一座，明隆庆年间（公元 1567——1572 年），木塔倒毁，万历三十七年（公元 1609年）重修这十三级八棱砖塔落成。一九八一年八月二十四日，该塔因地基下沉及霪雨而倾圮。一九八七年，为重修此塔，省、市、县三级组成考古发掘队，配合工程对塔基进行发掘清理。

　　发掘工作从八七年二月中旬开始，十一月份结束。清理了地宫内所藏文物，建账立卡，并落实了各种保护措施。到目前为止，已发掘出明代圆形塔基遗址：东西直径 19米、南北直径 20 米。塔基有环带形基槽深约 2.75 米～2.90 米，与明代的八棱形塔身相符；发掘出唐代方形塔基遗址，塔基以石条围边，每边长 26 米。在石条围边之内，发现19 个柱础，除南边为 5 个外，其余 3 边各有 6 个柱础。另外，在上述迴廊柱础所形成的规范之内，又发现四个承重柱柱础。这就是倒毁于明隆庆年间的顶复琉璃瓦的唐代方形木塔。经过全队人员的共同努力，业已圆满地完成了田野发掘的任务，取得了十分可喜的成绩。

　　法门寺地宫是我国迄今发现的佛塔地宫中最大的一座。地宫位于塔基之中，全长21.2 米，总面积为 31.48 平方米，包括踏步漫道、平台、隧道、前室、中室、后室及后室小龛等七部分。地宫由汉白玉和石灰石板构筑而成。值得庆幸的是，自唐懿宗咸通十五年（公元 874 年）正月四日封闭后，地宫未经后世扰动过。

　　在隧道中发现了《大唐咸通启送岐阳真身志文》和《监送真身使随真身供养道具及金

银宝器衣物帐》两通石碑。碑中详细记载了地宫沿革，懿、僖间迎送真身的盛况和物品名称、数量及奉献者姓名。后者是国内外现存篇幅最长、物主最多、品类最繁的物帐，实属十分珍贵的史料。

地宫内珍藏了数量众多的唐代文物，其中一类是佛指舍利，共四枚；另一类是为迎送舍利而奉献的金银宝器、珠玉、琉璃器、瓷器及丝织衣物等。其中金银器皿一百二十一件、组，琉璃器二十件、瓷器十六件、石质器具十二件、铁质器十六件、漆木及乐器十九件、珠玉、宝石等约四百件、颗，还有大批丝织物品。

金银器皿，富丽堂皇，璀灿夺目，堪称唐代金银器之大观。其中多数是懿宗和僖宗对佛的供养品，如鎏金珍珠装捧真身菩萨像，是为祈求懿宗"圣寿万春"而造的。许多刻划有"五哥"字样的器物，则均为僖宗对佛的供养品，这是迄今发现的确属唐代皇室所有的等级最高的金银器。大量的供养器物和佛教法器是这次考古发掘的重大收获之一。象鎏金鸳鸯团花双耳圈足银盆，素面银香案，仰莲瓣水碗、素面高圈足银灯盏等即属此类。法器中的锡杖共发现三支，以"迎真身银金花十二环锡杖"最为重要。其杖身中空，表面錾刻有缘觉十二僧。杖长 1960 毫米，比现藏于日本正仓院最大的白铜头锡杖的制作要精，等级要高。有些金银器物是皇帝为迎送真身而专门制造的。因此，上面多有錾文，刻明奉献时间、名称、重量、质地、件数、制作方法、监制者姓名及职位等项，内容丰富，史料价值极高。为研究唐代官廷内金银作坊组织、职官设置、度量衡制度及器物定名等方面的问题，提供了珍贵的资料。此次发掘，新发现的器类较多，如僖宗供养的三足架盐台、金银丝结条笼子、鎏金茶槽子、茶罗子、银锅轴等，对了解唐代贵族生活及社会风貌，均属难得的实物资料。从其工艺水平、造型特征上看，亦属难得的珍品。

这次发现的琉璃器，或洁如凝霜，或清如澄水，或温润其质，或玲珑其态。盘、碟、碗、托、瓶等，品类较多；蓝、黄、绿、白各色俱全，形制优美，花色绚丽。有的颇富西亚风格，有的则是地道的"唐品"，既反映了唐代中西文化频繁的联系，又为研究当时中国琉璃（玻璃）器的制造提供了十分珍贵的实物资料。

懿宗供养的一批秘色瓷，十分精美。为鉴定这种瓷器的时代和特点提供了一批标准器，解决了中国陶瓷史上长期以来悬而未决的问题。这批瓷器，是中国陶瓷史上的一项突破性发现。

这次发掘的又一重大收获是出土了大量精美的丝织品。据《物帐》记载，懿宗、僖宗、惠安皇太后等供养的各类纺织品达七百多件。但由于地宫保存条件较差，有些已损破成渣，有些已滥成灰，有些尚可抢救，一部分保存完好。现存部分虽然尚未一一与《物帐》勘对核实，但从已掌握的标本看，亦属考古史上具有划时代意义的发现。据初步观察，丝物品种有锦、绫、罗、纱、绢、绮、绣等类。夹金织物极为丰富，其中唐代织金锦则属首次发现。刺绣品的加工工艺多种多样，有蹙金绣、平绣、贴金绣、贴金加绣、绣加绘金等。特别是为"捧真身菩萨"制作的蹙金绣袄、金花袈裟、案裙、拜垫等衣、物保存完好，俨然如新，表现了唐代丝织方面的惊人技艺。这一批几乎涉及唐代全部丝织物品精华的发现，不但为研究中国古代服饰史、纺织史和织造技术史提供了重要的实物证据，从中也可看出我国丝织品在当时世界上产生巨大影响的原因。

此外，还发现一批精美的石刻造像，木雕及首饰等。

值得特别指出的是，发现了保存完好的四枚佛指舍利。经与《志文》及有关文献勘验，确系唐代皇帝多次迎送的释迦牟尼佛的真身舍利。据现在所知，这是世界上仅存的佛指舍利。它的发现实为佛教世界中一件值得庆幸的大事。

第一枚舍利，安置于地宫后室，贮于唐懿宗供奉的八重宝函之中。宝函两侧有石刻天王护持。八重函的最外层为银棱盝顶檀香木宝函，出土时已朽破，尚未修复。其余七重由外及里是：鎏金四天王盝顶宝函、素面盝顶银函、鎏金如来说法银宝函、纯金六臂观音盝顶宝函、金筐宝钿珍珠装金宝函、金筐宝钿珍珠装珷玞石函、宝珠顶单檐四门纯金塔。这枚佛指是在五月五日（阴历四月初八）凌晨一时清理宝函时发现的。其长40.3毫米、宽17.55～20.11毫米、腔径13.75毫米～16.5毫米，重16.2克，套置于塔基之银柱上。

第二枚佛指舍利，安置于地宫中室汉白玉双檐灵帐之中。五月九日晨取出。

第三枚佛指舍利，秘藏于地宫后室小龛内的铁函之内，函外用夹金织物包裹。函内还套装有四重宝函，最外层是鎏金四十五尊造像盝顶宝函，其上錾刻有"奉为皇帝敬造释迦牟尼佛真身宝函"等字样。函内放一檀香木函，再内是水晶椁，椁盖两端有黄、蓝宝石各一，周围镶以珍珠。安置舍利的玉棺套在椁内。五月十日晨将其揭开，使这枚舍利重现人间。

第四枚佛指舍利安置在地宫前室的彩绘四铺菩萨舍利塔中，正月十二日将其揭开，发现了舍利。

据有关史籍记载：北魏时即有开启地宫供养舍利之事。唐代的高宗、武后、中宗、肃宗、德宗、宪宗、懿宗诸朝均将舍利迎入宫中，多殊礼，其中尤以后二者最为隆盛。有唐一代，迎送真身是皇室活动中的一件大事。懿宗十四年（公元873年）迎真身入宫中，朝野惊动，盛况空前。"珊瑚、玛瑙、珍珠、瑟瑟缀为幡幢"，"剪采为幡为伞"，约以万队。都城士庶，奔走云集，自开元门达于岐川，车马昼夜相属，饮馔盈溢路衢。四月八日迎入长安，自开远门安福楼，赡礼之士女，道从之僧徒，如潮如流；歌舞管弦，梵诵之声，沸盈天地。未几，懿宗驾崩，僖宗即位，佛指舍利送回法门寺。参与这次送真身活动的，除皇室贵族外，还有十几位大德高僧亲躬其事。其中见于典籍的有左右街僧录清澜、彦楚、首座僧彻、大教三藏遍觉法师智慧轮等人。尤其是智慧轮法师，与日本高僧圆珍，圆仁过从甚密，曾馈赠给后二人不少经典秘籍。在中日文化交流史上被传为佳话。随同这些高僧恭送真身的还有中天竺沙门僧伽提和，僖宗因其殊功，予以"赐紫归本国"的隆遇。所以，唐代懿、僖间迎送真身的活动，可以说是一次颇有影响的国际间的盛会。

法门寺地宫，堪称荟萃唐代文物的宝库。其中文物数量之多，品类之繁、质量之高，保存之完好，在唐代考古上是空前的。这批文物等级最高，历史背景清楚，纪年明确，是唐代物质文化高度发达的集中表现。不论在社会政治史、文化史、宗教史、科技史，还是中外交流史美术史等方面的研究上，都具有极为重要的学术价值。从这个意义上说，它的发现，无疑是世界文化史上的一件幸事。这一发现将与秦兵马俑坑，马王堆汉墓等重大发现一样光耀史册。

在发掘过程中，国家文物局十分关怀，省政府常务委员会曾两次开会讨论有关事宜，省、市、县各级领导极为重视，亲临现场指导和督促。法门寺地宫文物的发现，提供了发展我省西线旅游事业的重大突破口。有了这个龙头，会较快地促进扶、岐、凤、宝西线旅游点的建设，对贯彻国务院关于"加强保护，改善管理，搞好改革，充分发挥文物的作用，继承和发扬民族优秀的文化传统，为社会主义服务，为人民服务，为建设具有中国特色的社会主义作出贡献"的方针，具有重大意义。法门寺这批绚丽多彩的文化珍品，具有鲜明的民族特色，它是了解和认识我国民族文化艺术传统的重要资料。它所展示的各种传统艺术形式，可以为我们今天批判地继承历史文化遗产，创造社会主义的民族新文化提供借鉴。

这部图册是在省政府、省文物局领导同志的热情关怀和支持下进行的，由法门寺考古队同志共同研究选编的。参加工作的同志有韩伟、任周芳、韩金科、淮建邦、王占奎、曹玮、傅升岐和金宪镛等同志，照片是由王保平同志负责拍摄的。图版的编排和设计是由陕西人民美术出版社邵梦龙同志负责的，由韩伟、金宪镛、王保平选集定稿，在这里应对他们的有意义的劳动，表示感谢。我们希望这本图册的出版，有益于文博考古事业的发展，通过图册的反映，使人们对法门寺文物有更多更深刻的认识，对祖国历史文化遗产更加爱护和重视，在宏扬民族优秀文化传统方面，在建设具有中国特色的社会主义新文化方面有所助益，这就达到了我们所期望的目的。

1988 年 3 月 5 日于西安

INTRODUCTION

Shi Xingbang

In 1987 , during the excavation of the crypt under the ruined stupa at Famen Temple , archeologists brought to light a large number of historical relics. These finds are of great value in the study of the religion , technology and society of the Tang Dynasty , and hence have aroused great attention of people of various social circles and academic fields. In order to make these priceless relics public and meet the urgent needs of the academic circles and general readers at an early date , we have compiled this selection of the pictures of some representative relics unearthed from the Famen Temple crypt , before a detailed report is officially published.

Famen Temple , one of the famous monasteries keeping the genuine sarira of Sakyamuni in China , is located at the Town of Famen , 10 kilometers north of Fufeng County and 120 kilometers northwest of Xi′an , China′s famous ancient capital. According to historical records , the temple was built during the reigns of Emperors Huan and Ling (147−189) of the Eastern Han Dyansty and was later credited with the title of "Father of Temples and Pagodas in Central Shaanxi". The temple witnessed its heyday in the Tang times. During the years of Longqing (1567−1572) of the Ming Dynasty , the four−storeyed wooden stupa in the temple , built in the Tang times , collapsed. In the thirty−seventh year of Wanli (1609) of Ming , a thirteen−storeyed octagonal brick stupa was built on the very site of the former stupa. On August 24 , 1981 , the brick stupa crumbled owing to the successive rains and the sinking of its base. In 1987 , an archeological team was formed of experts from Fufeng County , Baoji City and Shaanxi Province to excavate the ruins of the stupa as a preparatory operation for the rebuilding of the stupa.

The excavation lasted Fabruary through November , 1987. The discovery of the crypt under the base of the ruined stupa is the most important result of the operation. The archeologists unearthed from the crypt a large number of percious relics , sorted them out , filed them in a catalog , and took all protective measures for their preservation. So far , the archaeologists have revealed the Tang stupa′s base and the Ming stupa′s base. The Ming stupa′s base is roughly circular , 19 meters from east to west and 20 meters from north to south , with an octangular base slot 2.75−2.90 meters deep. The Tang stupa′s base is 26 meters square , edged with stone bars. Inside the stone bars along the four sides are found 19 pillar bases , 5 of which are on the south side. Further inside are revealed 4 larger pillar bases. With the joint efforts of the team members , the field operation has already come to a successful and fruitful end.

The crypt at Famen Temple is the largest of its kind ever discovered in China. It lies under the base of the stupa , with a length of 21.2 meters and a total floor space of 31.48 square meters. The stupa consists of seven parts:an approach , a landing , a tunnel , front , middle and rear chambers and a niche. The crypt is built of white marble and limestone slabs. Luckily , it has never been disturbed ever since it was closed on the fourth day of the first month (in lunar calender) of the fifteenth year of Xiantong under the reign of Tang Emperor Xizong ,

Found in the tunnel are two inscribed stone tablets. One of them bears a text with the title " Escorting Sakyamuni′s Genuine Sarira to Famen Temple in the Years of Xiantong of the Tang Dynasty". The other is "List of Gold , Silver and Other Precious Articles and Silk Fabrics Contributed to Worship Sakyamuni′s Genuine Sarira". The two tablets carry a detailed description of the building of the crypt and the grand occasions of welcoming the sarira to the court and escorting it back to the stupa during Emperors Yizong and Xizong′s times , as well as a complete list of the contributed articles and the names of the contributors.Especially worth mentioning is the list,which is the longest of its kind,containing the greatest variety of articles and most numerous owners,ever found in China and abroad.Hence,it is a set of invaluable historical data.

The relics unearthed from the crypt fall into two categories:one is the sarira—four pieces of Sakyamuni's finger bones ,the other are the contributed articles—gold and silver articles ,gems ,glassware ,porcelainware and silk fabrics.There are 121 pieces of gold and silver articles ,20 pieces of glassware ,16 pieces of porcelainware ,12 pieces of stoneware ,16 pieces of ironware ,pearls ,and a large quantity of silk fabrics.

The gold and silver articles,gorgeous and resplendent,are a grand display of the high technology and craftsmanship of the Tang Dynasty.Majority of these articles were offered by Emperors Yizong and Xizong to worship Buddha.A statue of the Bodhisattva to carry Buddha's sarira was offered to pray to Buddha for Emperor Yizong's long life.Some articles bearing the inscription "五哥" were contributed by Emperor Xizong to worship Buddha.These are the verified gold and silver articles of Tang emperors,the highest ranking of this category ever found.

Another major yield of this excavation is the large number of articles contributed to worship Buddha or used in Buddhist service.Examples of the former type are a silver tub with gilded patterns of posy and mandarin ducks ,a plain—face silver incense—burner table, a lotus—flower—shaped silver bowl and a plain—face ,ring—foot silver lamp.Examples of the latter type are three monk's staffs.The best of the three is a gold and silver staff with twelve rings linked in a single wheel at the top.Its hollow shaft is decorated with twelve images of monks on its surface.This staff ,1.96 m long ,exceeds in size ,quality and rank the copper—nickel—top staff ,Japan's largest Buddhist monk's staff ,kept in the Shosoin treasure house.

Some of the gold and silver articles were specially made on the order of the emperors to be offered to Buddha on the occasion of greeting or sending—off Buddha's sarira.Therefore ,the articles mostly bear the inscriptions noting the dates of their offering ,their names ,weights ,numbers ,materials ,manufacturing techniques ,supervisors' names and offical titles ,etc.These inscriptions,so rich in content,are themselves very important historical data for the study of the court's gold and silver workshops ,the institution of manufacturing supervisors ,the systems of weights and measures and the terminology of the articles of the Tang Dynasty.

This excavation also yields some new finds ,such as a salt basin with a tripod.a cage woven with braids of fine gold and silver strands ,and a set of tea processing tools (including a wheel—shaped grinding roller ,a crescent—shaped grinding mortar and a tea sifter) — all offered by Emperor Xizong.These new finds are invaluable material data for our understanding of the life of the nobility and the social customs of the Tang times.They are also superb in craftsmanship and design.

The glass vessels discovered from the crypt are pure as frost ,or transparent as clean water ,fine in quality and exquisite in design.In addition ,they are rich in variety —the plate ,the dish ,the bowl ,the tray ,the vase ,etc ,and varied in color — blue ,yellow ,green ,white ,etc.Some are very much of the West Asian style;some are typically of the Chinese style of the Tang times.Such a mix eloquently reflects the booming cultural exchanges between China and the Western Regions during those days.The finds also provide precious material data for the study of the history of the manufacturing of Chinese glassware.

The secret porcelain vessels offered by Emperor Yizong are extremely fine and exquisite ,and extremely important for the resolution of an outstanding question in the history of Chinese ceramics.The so—called secret porcelain was recorded in historical books and has been much talked about by scholars.Nevertheless,no secret porcelainware has ever been discovered until the present find.Therefore ,this discovery means a breakthrough ,and these secret porcelain vessels are legitimately to serve as the standards for the identification of this kind of porcelainware.

The large quantity of fine and exquisite silk fabrics are also an important yield of this excavation.According to the List of contributed articles inscribed on the stone tablet,the number of silk fabrics offered by Emperors Yizong and Xizong,Empress Dowager Hui'an and others amounts to more than 700 (pieces).However,owing to the unfavorable conditions of the crypt,many of the fabrics have already decayed to fragments and even to ashes.Some are still recoverable.And some are preserved in good condition.A preliminary study shows that these fabrics include brocade,twill,leno,gauze,pongee,embroidered and printed silk.This is the first time fabrics woven with the combined silk and gold thread have been found.An embroidered coat,a golden flower Kasaya,a hassock and other pieces presented to the Bodhisattava to carry Sakyamuni's sarira are in good condition.In exquisite designs of flowers and clouds,these pieces display the astonishing weaving techniques of the Tang Dynasty.The discovery of almost a complete variety of Tang silk fabrics has provided physical data for the study of the history of ancient China's costume,textile and weaving technique.The discovery also helps to account for China's great reputation of her silks in the world of those times.

In addition to the above finds,there are a number of fine stone sculptures,wooden sculptures and ornaments unearthed from the crypt.

Of special importance is the discovery of the four well—preserved Sakyamuni's finger bones.Having checked the inscription on the stone tablets and related historical records,the archeologists have identified these bones as Sakyamuni's genuine relics which the Tang emperors welcomed to the capital and sent back to the stupa many times.These bones,as far as we know,are the only recovery of Sakyamuni's relics in the world.Hence,their discovery is really a happy event of great significance for the Buddhist world.

The first finger bone was discovered in a stupa—shaped casket covered by seven successively bigger ones put in the rear chamber of the crypt.The caskets were offered by the Tang Emperor Yizong.The outermost casket is made of sandal—wood,which is already rotten upon the discovery.The inner seven are (from outside to inside) respectively:the gilded silver casket with four Devarajas' images,the silver casket with design—free surface,the gilded silver casket with the image of Tathagata preaching Buddhism,the pure gold casket with the image of six—armed Avalokitesvara,the pure gold casket decorated with pearls,the marble casket decorated with gems and pearls,and the pure gold casket in the shape of a stupa.

The second finger bone was found in a white marble double—eared alcove on the morning of May 9.

The third was discovered in a small iron casket placed in the niche in the rear chamber,wrapped in gold color silk.The bone was placed inside four caskets.The outermost casket with 45 gilded images is engraved with the words:" This precious casket which contains the genuine finger bone of Sakyamuni is presented by Tang Emperor." When the casket was opened,a smaller sandalwood casket was revealed inside.Further inside,there was a crystal casket inlaid with a yellow gem at one end and a blue gem at the other,each surrounded by pearls.The bone itself was in a jade box,and was brought to light on the morning of May 10.

The fourth finger bone was obtained from a painted sarira stupa in the front chamber of the crypt May 12.

According to historical records,the practice of bringing Buddhist sarira out of the crypt for worshiping can be traced back as early as the Northern Wei Dynasty.During the Tang times,quite a few emperors,such as Gaozong,Zhongzong,Suzong,Xianzong and Yizong,and Empress Wu Zetian,were all devout Buddhist believers,who welcomed the sarira of Sakyamuni to the capital for worshiping.The ceremony of welcoming the sarira was a spectacular event in the Tang times.The fourteenth year of the reign of Emperor Yizong witnessed an especially grand occasion of this kind.Thousands and thousands of people lined up on both sides of the road leading from Famen Temple to the capital Chang'an.Sakyamuni's sarira was under the escort of high—ranking officials,Buddhist monks and worshippers.carrying banners and streamers of various colors,and precious articles like corals,gems and pearls.Horses and chariots ran in endless succession.Food and drinks were offered all along the route.On the eighth day of the fourth month (of the lunar calender) when the sarira was escorted into the city monks and spectators,men and women,flooded the sidewalks from the Kaiyuan Gate to the Anfu Tower while music and chants soared to the sky.Shortly after,Emperor Yizong died and Emperor Xizong succeeded to the throne,who held another grand ceremony to escort the sarira back to Famen Temple.Also attending the ceremonies were a dozen or so high—ranking monks,such as Luqinglan,Yanchu and Zhihuilun,and some monks from India and other countries.Therefore,these ceremonies themselves were influential cultural activities of international significance.

The Famen Temple crypt is justified to be credited with the title of the treasury of Tang cultural relics.The articles unearthed form the crypt excel in quantity,quality,variety and the condition of preservation all the previous finds in Tang archeology.These relics,together with the invaluable inscriptions they bear provide extremely significant physical data for the study of the politics,culture,religion,science and technology,fine art and international exchanges of the Tang Dynasty.This discovery,therefore,is undoubtedly a lucky and great event in the history of world culture.It is another brilliant archeological feat,following the discovery of the Qin terra—cotta warriors and horses and that of the Han Tomb at Mawangdui.

During the course of the excavation,the national Adiministration of Cultural Relics offered great support and timely guidance.Shaanxi Provincial Government held two special meetings to discuss the matter.Leading personnel from the province,Baoji City and Fufeng County went in person to the field and gave the team good helps and advice.

The discovery of the Famen Temple crypt is of great significance to the development of the fine tradition of great Chinese culture and the building of China's socialist civilization.Besides,it has opened up a new spot of great attractiveness for tourism,which will necessarily help develop the cultural exchanges with foreign countries today as it once did in history.

This album is prepared by Han Wei,Ren Zhoufang,Huai Jianbang,Han Jinke,Wang Zhankui,Cao Wei,Fu Shengqi and Jin Xianyong of the Archeological Team of Famen Temple,with Han Wei,Jin Xianyong and Wang Baoping as the editors,Wang Baoping as the photographer and Shao Menglong as the editor and binding designer.We are deeply indebted to the Provincial Government of Shaanxi and its Bureau of Culture,and Shaanxi People's Fine Arts Publishing House,whose support and cooperation are indispensable for the publication of this work.

Finally we expect that the publication of this album will benefit the development of archeology and culture,help readers acquire a better understanding of the relics unearthed from the Famen Temple crypt,enhance people's love and care for our historical and cultural heritage,and promote the building of China's new culture of socialism.

Xi'an,Shaanxi

March 5,1988

目　录

法门寺地宫唐代文物图版

Contents

The Photos of the Tang Relics Discovered in the Crypt of Famen Femple.

1.法门寺鸟瞰

2. 中国佛教协会会长赵朴初兴致勃勃地参观法门寺

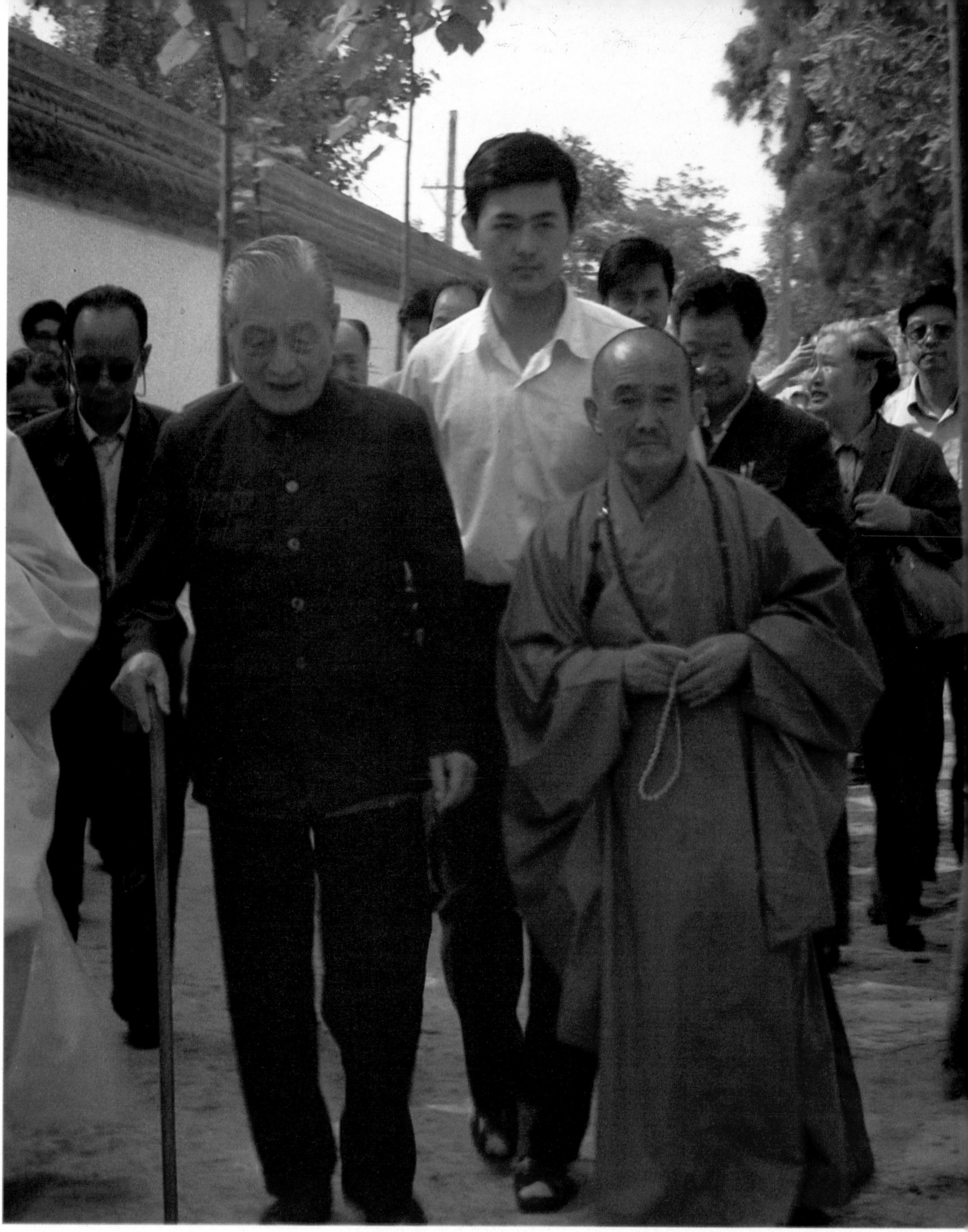

3. 僧众在做法事

4.法门寺殿宇内景

5. 殿宇内塑的十八罗汉

殿宇内塑的十八罗汉

6.殿宇内塑的普贤菩萨

7.殿宇内塑的文殊菩萨

8.殿宇内塑的红孩儿

9.传说中的明代民女宋巧姣告状跪石处

11. 席棚遮盖的下面即发掘地宫处

12. 唐代地宫大门

13. 唐代地宫大门未开启时之原状

14. 唐代地宫大门的双凤楣额

15.考古工作者清理地宫中室的佛指舍利(图一)

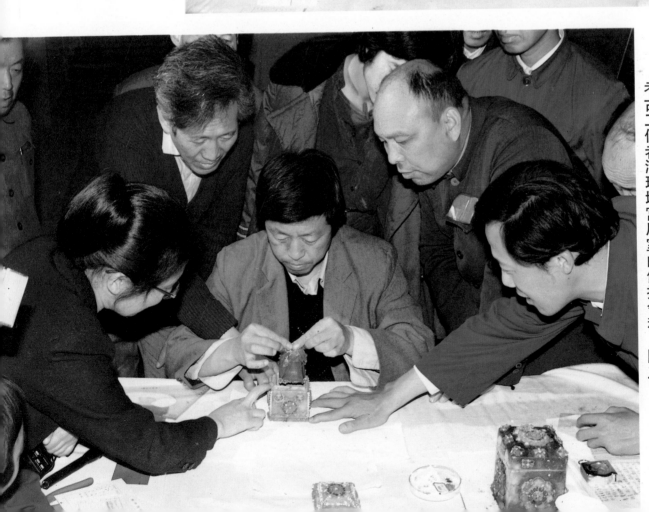

考古工作者清理地宫前室的佛指舍利 （图二）

考古工作者清理地宫后室的佛指舍利 （图三）

1.鎏金双鸳团花银盆

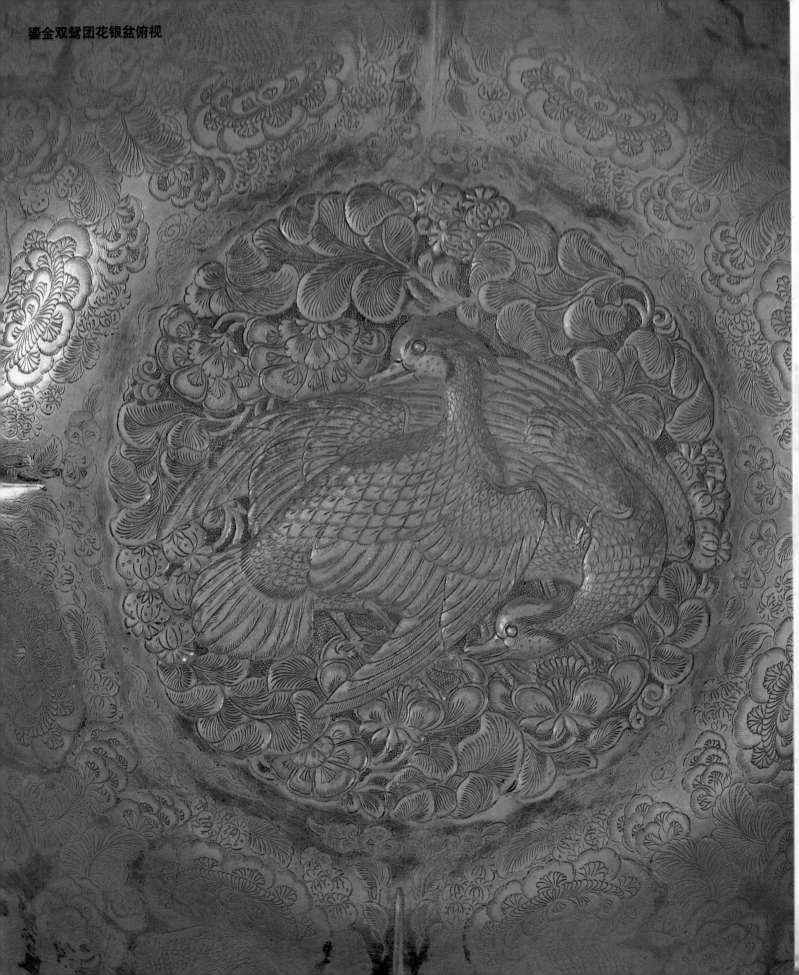

2.鎏金双凤衔绶带御前赐银方盒

金双凤衔绶带御前赐银方盒俯视

4.鎏金双狮纹菱弧形圈足银盒

3.鎏金银龟盒

鎏金双狮纹菱弧形圈足银盒俯视

5.椭方形素面银盒

6.素面圈足银盒

7.双鸿纹海棠形银盒

8.十字三钴杵铜盒

9.鎏金壶门座波罗子

鎏金人物画银坛子局部

鎏金十字折枝花小银碟（平底）

鎏金十字折技花小银碟（圈足）

鎏金十字折技花小银碟俯视

15、鎏金壶门座鸿雁纹五环银熏炉

17. 鎏金鸿雁纹镂孔银香囊（小）
鎏金双蜂团花纹镂孔银香囊（大）

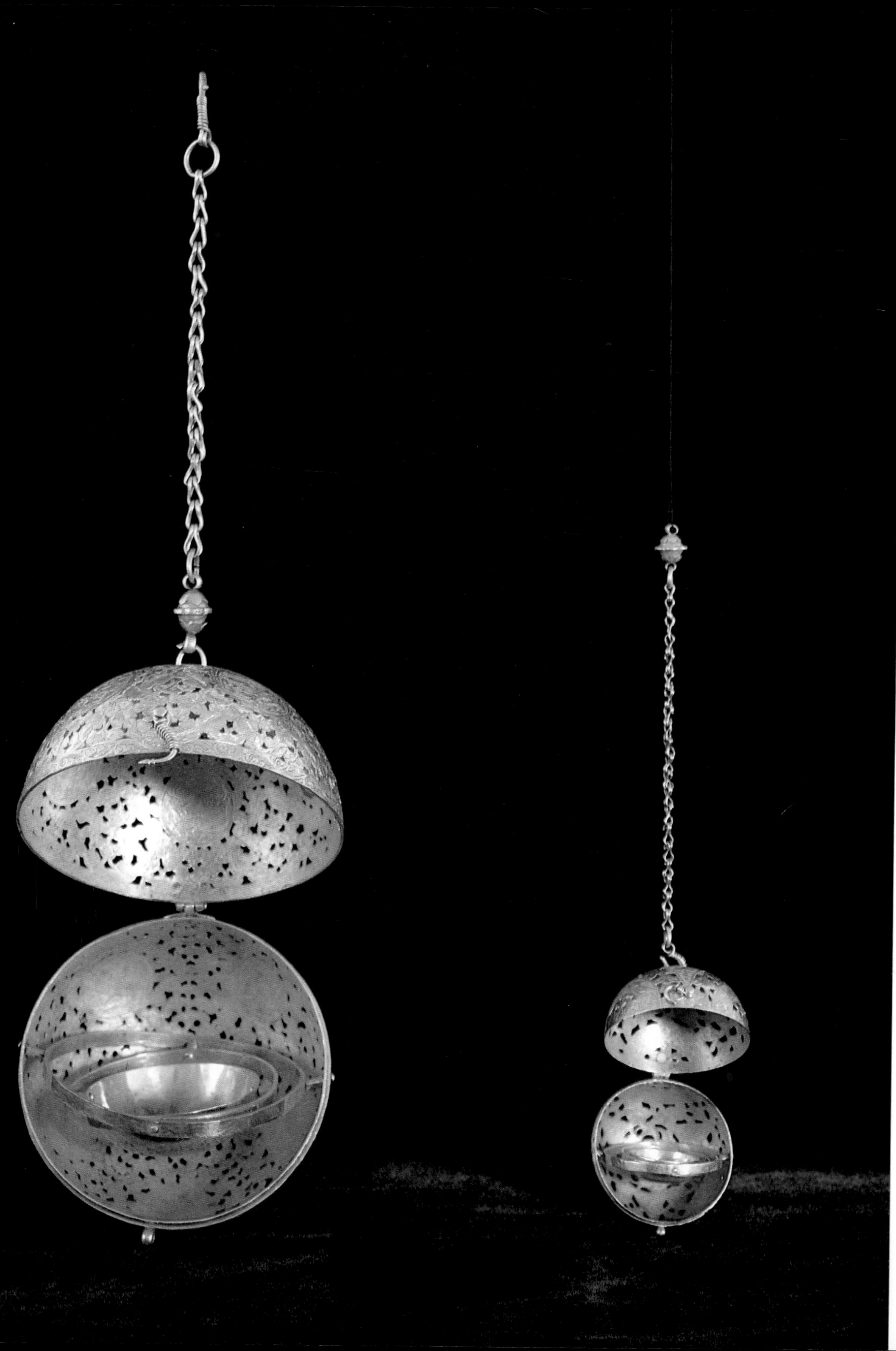

鎏金鸿雁纹镂孔银香囊（小）打开状

鎏金双蜂团花纹镂孔银香囊（大）打开状

鎏金双蜂团花纹镂孔银香囊(局部)

鎏金鸿雁纹镂孔银香囊(局部)

鎏金仙人驾鹤纹壶门座茶罗子打开状

十

20.纯银锅轴

鎏金 壺门座茶碾子打开后上置纯银锅轴

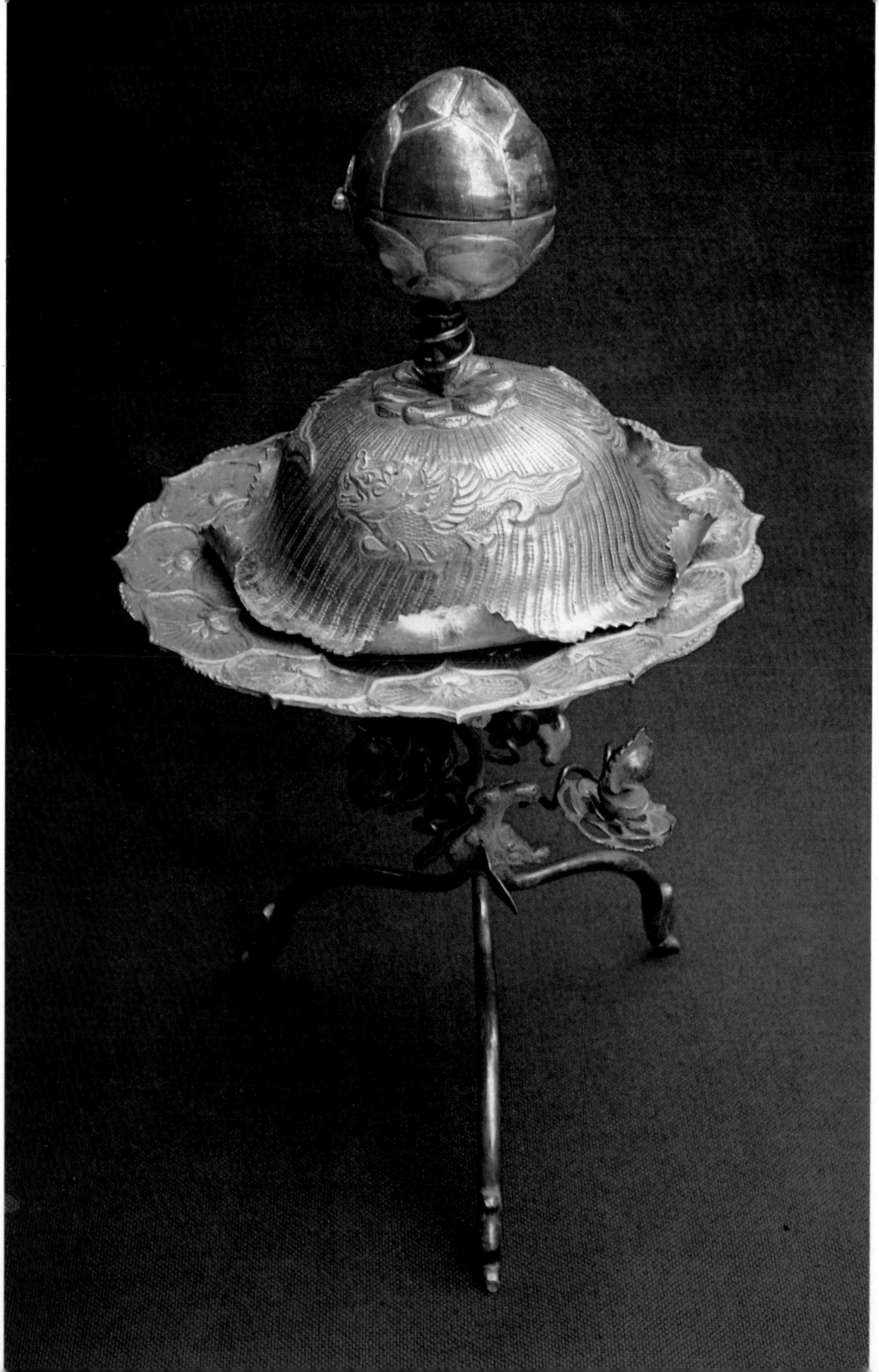

21.摩羯纹蕾钮三足盐台

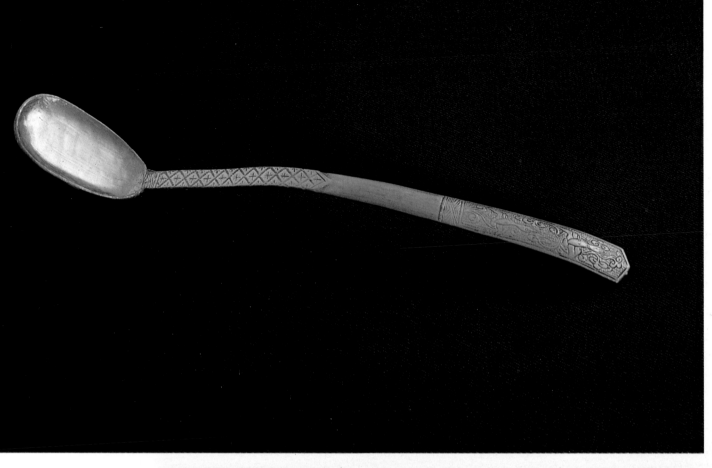

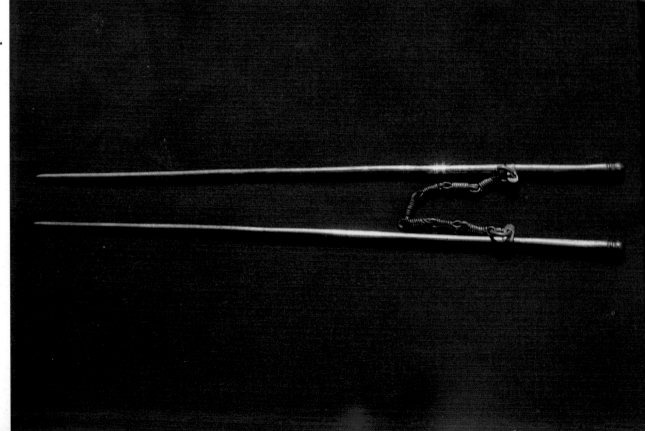

24.
系链银火筋

25. 捧真身菩萨

捧真身菩萨侧面观

捧真身菩萨底座局部（一）

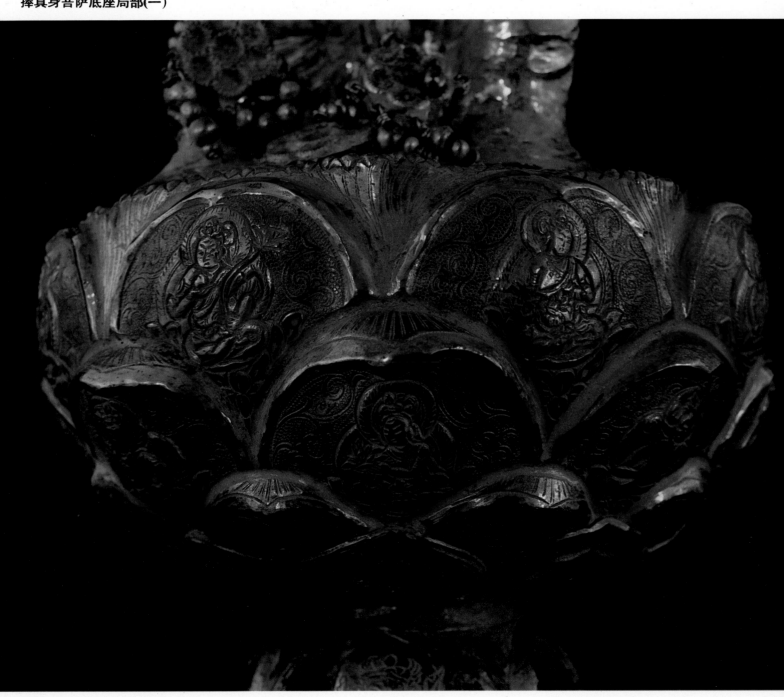

捧真身菩萨底座局部(二)

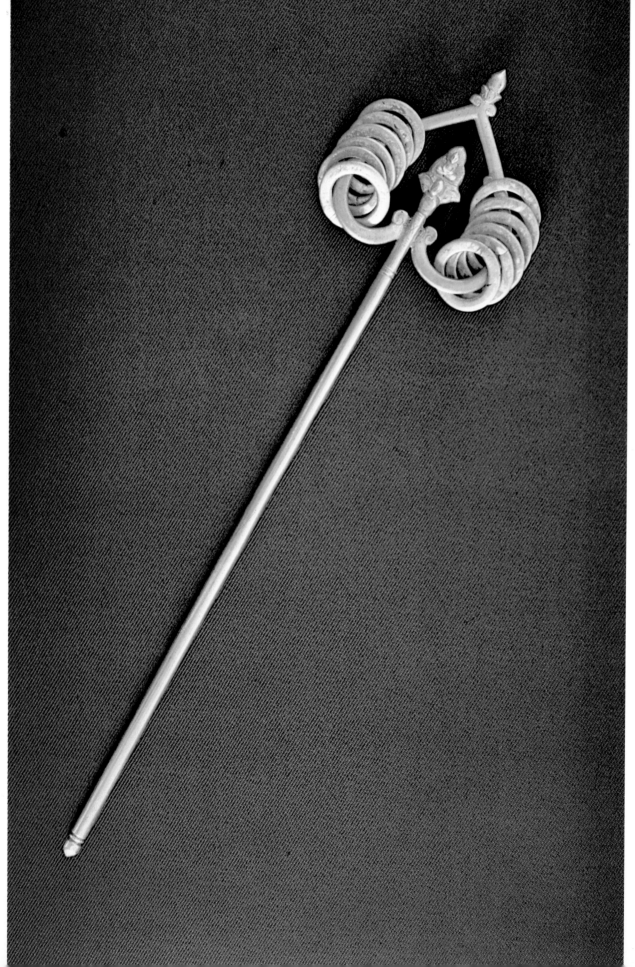

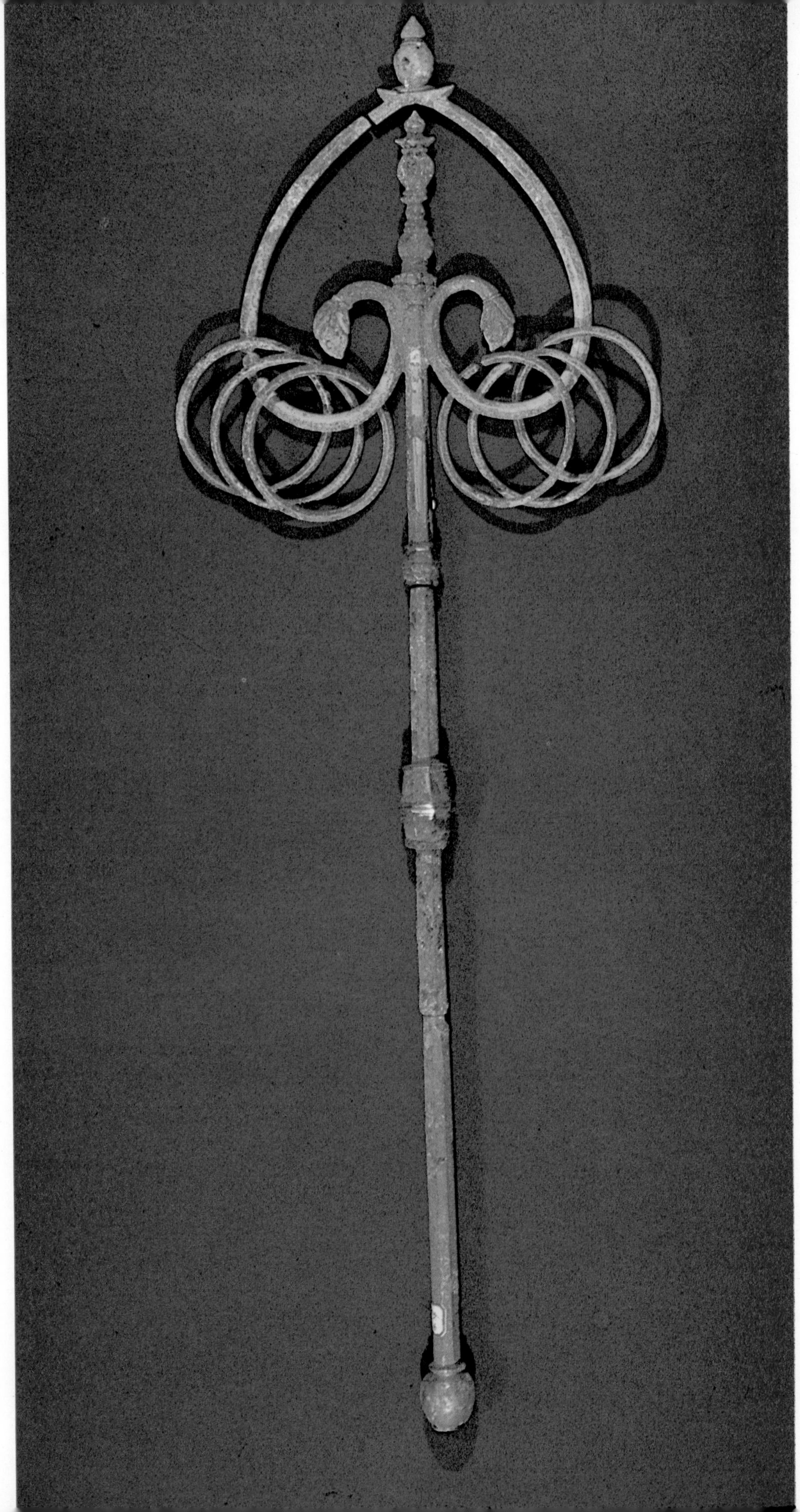

28.
鎏金单轮六环铜锡杖

银金花双轮十二环锡杖局部

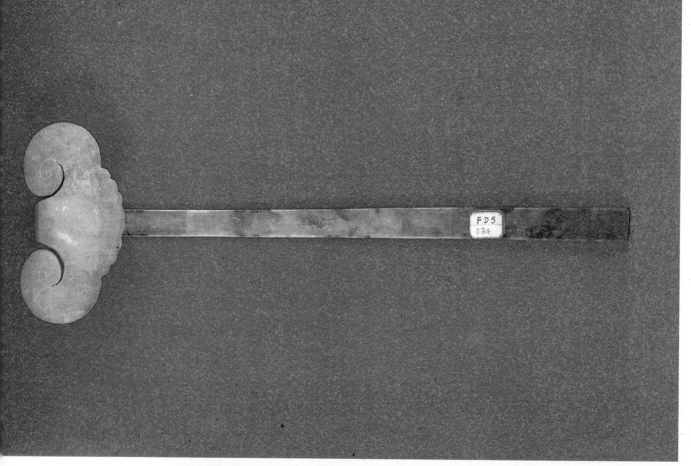

31. 鎏金三钴杵纹臂钏

32.纯金迎真身钵盂

33.鎏金团花银钵盂

34.银芙蕖

36.盘圆座葵口小银碟

38.鎏金仰莲瓣荷叶圈足银碗

鎏金仰莲瓣荷叶圈足银碗底部

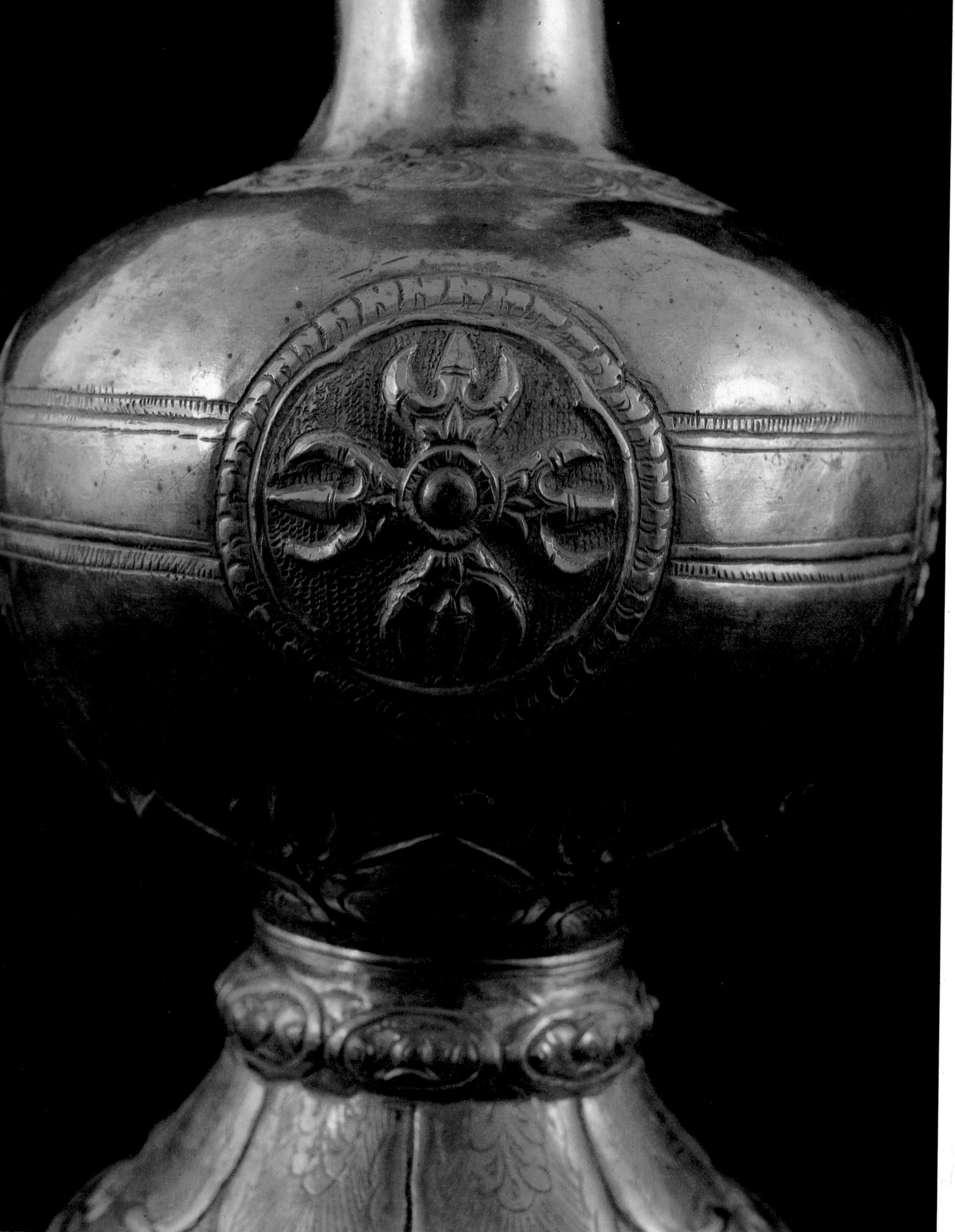

鎏金三钴杵纹银阏伽瓶局部

40.双凤纹鎏金银棺

46.金筐宝钿珍珠装珷玞石盝顶宝函

金筐宝钿珍珠装□□石盝顶宝函局部

刚出土打开包裹的宝珠顶单檐纯金四门塔

48.宝珠顶单檐纯金四门塔内供养的佛指舍利

49.刻花蓝琉璃盘

刻花蓝琉璃盘俯视

50.描金刻花蓝琉璃盘

描金刻花蓝琉璃盘俯视

54.琥珀狻猊(一)

琥珀狻猊(二)

55.水晶枕

56.随球

汉白玉浮雕绘彩阿育王塔局部(一)

汉白玉浮雕绘彩阿育王塔局部（二）

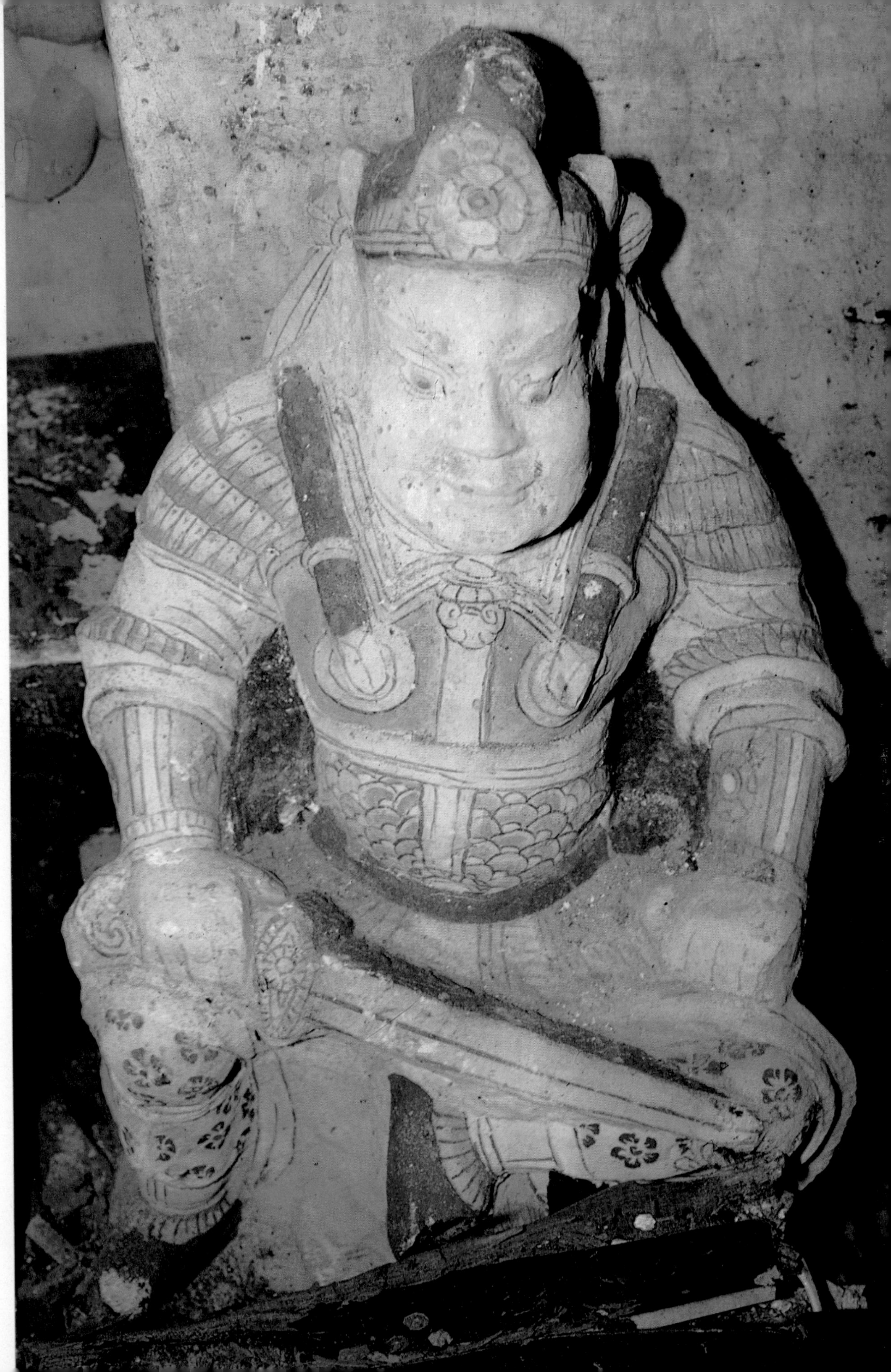

59. 石刻南方天王

60. 石刻东方天王

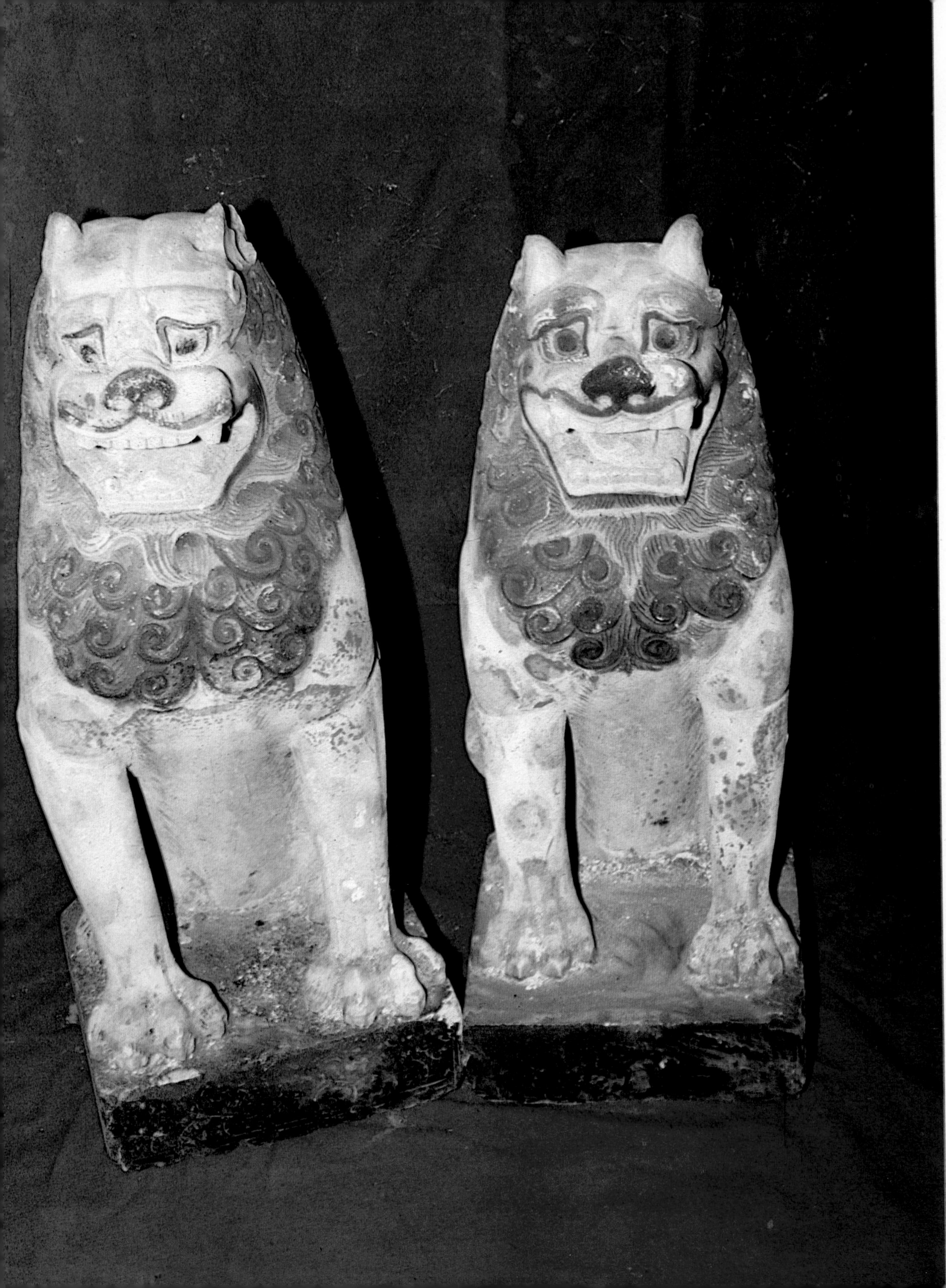

61.
彩绘金毛双狮

图 版 解 说

1、鎏金双鸳团花银盆

浇铸成型，花纹錾刻，纹饰鎏金，鱼子纹底。盆为葵瓣形侈口，圆唇，斜腹下收，矮圈足。盆口錾一周莲瓣纹，盆壁分为四瓣，每瓣錾两个阔叶石榴团花，团花中有一只鼓翼鸳鸯立于仰莲座上，两两相对，余白衬以流云和三角阔叶纹。盆腹内外花纹雷同，犹如渗透一样。盆底类似浅浮雕，以一对嬉戏鸳鸯为中心的阔叶石榴大团花。盆外两侧各铆接两个前额刻"王"字的天龙铺首，口衔饰有海棠花的圆环，环上套接弓形提耳。圈足微外撇，外饰二十四朵莲花。盆底外壁錾"浙西"二字。通高 145 毫米，口径 460 毫米，足径 285 毫米，足高 25 毫米，壁厚 6 毫米。总重 6265 克。

2、鎏金双凤衔绶带御前赐银方盒

钣金成型，纹饰鎏金。盒体呈扁方形，直壁，浅腹，平底，短圈足。盖、身上下对称，以子母口扣合。隆盖面边缘饰莲瓣一周，中心为口衔绶带相对翱翔的双凤团花，角隅錾十字绶带花结纹样。盒侧上下散点错列一字形扁团花，盒底内外有同心圆旋痕。圈足与盒身焊接。盖面墨书"随真身御前赐"六字。通高 95 毫米，边长 215 毫米，圈足高 17 毫米，足径 180 毫米。总重 1585 克。

3、鎏金银龟盒

分体钣金、焊接成型。龟状，昂首，曲尾，四足内缩，以背甲作盖，内焊椭圆形子口架，尾与龟腹焊接。各部位纹饰与龟体相近，形象逼真。通高 130 毫米，长 280 毫米，宽 150 毫米。

4、鎏金双狮纹菱弧形圈足银盒

钣金成型，纹饰鎏金。盒体呈菱弧状，直壁，浅腹，平底，喇叭形圈足。上下对称，以子母口扣合。盖缘饰一周莲瓣，盖面内以联珠组成一个菱形，与周边呈相斗布局。内菱形中部錾两只腾跃的狮子，四周衬以西番莲与缠枝蔓草。内外菱形的角隅饰背分式西番莲纹样，腹壁上下均錾二方连续的莲叶蔓草，圈足饰一周简化莲瓣。通高 120 毫米，口径 173×168 毫米，圈足高 24 毫米，足径 148×138 毫米。总重 799 克。

5、椭方形素面银盒

钣金成型，通体光素。盝顶盖，盖刹四周有凹棱，盖缘有宽 3 毫米的小平沿，直壁，浅腹、平底，矮圈足，通高 97 毫米，长径 173 毫米，短径 119 毫米。总重 605.5 克。

6、素面圈足银盒

钣金成型。直壁，浅腹，平底，圈足。盖面及盖底均有旋削痕迹，中心有顶眼，通体素净，外壁抛光。通高 98 毫米，直径 184 毫米，圈足高 21 毫米，足径 152 毫米。总重 816.5 克。

7、双鸿纹海棠形银盒

钣金成型，纹饰模冲。盒体呈海棠形。盖面隆起，模冲出一对首尾相对，振翅飞翔的鸿雁。通高 20 毫米，长 51 毫米，宽 36 毫米。总重 20 克。

8、十字三钴杵铜盒

钣金成型，纹饰錾刻。盖与身上下对称。盖面錾刻交叉成十字的三钴金刚杵纹样，通体绿锈。通高 51 毫米，径 104 毫米。总重 196.5 克。

9、鎏金壶门座波罗子

一套五件。均钣金成型，外腹鎏金，形制相同，各以子母口扣合。直口，浅腹，平底，壶门座圈足。器内底焊接十字形格架，圈足有镂空的六个壶门，壶门间饰背分式忍冬草。底外壁有同心圆旋痕。每层高 38.7 毫米，口径 102.8 毫米，座外径 112 毫米，腹深 11.9 毫米，个重 243 克，总重 1235 克。

10、鎏金人物画银坛子

钣金成型，纹饰鎏金。带盖，直口，深腹，平底，圈足。盖钮为宝珠形。盖面隆起，分为四瓣。每瓣内模冲出一只飞狮，细部施以錾刻，底部衬以缠枝蔓草。每瓣凹棱侧饰"S"状二方连续纹样。坛盖与身以子母口扣合，腹壁划分为四个壸门规范，其中分别錾仙人对弈，伯牙俸琴，箫史吹箫，金蛇吐珠等人物画。高 247 毫米，径 132 毫米，腹深 112 毫米，圈足径 126 毫米。总重 883.5 克。

11、鎏金伎乐纹调达子

钣金成型，纹饰涂金。带盖，直口，深腹，平底，圈足。盖作立沿，沿面饰一周二方连续的蔓草。盖面高隆，边缘錾水波与莲瓣纹，中心为一宝珠形钮，下衬一周莲瓣，座四周錾两只鸳鸯和一只飞禽，衬以蔓草。腹壁呈内弧，口沿饰一周蔓草。腹壁中部刻三名吹乐，舞蹈的伎乐并衬有蔓草，底部一周饰莲瓣。喇叭形圈足，上部有圆箍棱，棱上饰四出扁团花，下部錾莲叶叶脉纹。通高 117 毫米，盖口径 56 毫米，杯高 58 毫米，杯径 54 毫米，足径 63 毫米。总重 149.5 克。

12、鎏金带盖卷荷圈足银羹碗子

浇铸成型，纹饰涂金。由盖、碗子、碗托三部分组成。盖呈半球状，有莲蕾形钮，钮座为七瓣梅花，盖面饰镂空如意云头四朵，盖沿直立；碗子素净，平宽折沿，弧腹、圆底。碗托与圈足焊接，托外为模冲的双层仰莲瓣，圈足饰叶脉纹，呈卷荷状。通高 98 毫米，盖高 45 毫米，盖径 71 毫米，碗径 66.5 毫米，深 24 毫米，足高 27 毫米，足径 80 毫米。总重 213.5 克。

13、鎏金十字折枝花小银碟

钣金成形，纹饰涂金。共 20 件，有带圈足或无圈足之区别。五瓣葵口，浅腹。碟心为阔叶团花一朵，每瓣錾十字形折枝花一朵。平底：高 14 毫米，径 102 毫米。重 120 克。圈足：高 19 毫米，径 100 毫米。重 130 克。

14、鎏金卧龟莲花纹朵带五足银熏炉

钣金成型，附件浇铸，纹饰涂金。由炉盖，炉身组成。炉盖宽沿平下折，与炉身扣合。沿面錾饰背分式忍冬纹，高隆的盖面底缘饰莲瓣纹一周，面上有五朵莲花，每朵莲花上卧有一龟，龟首反顾，口衔瑞草，莲花以枝蔓相连绕。宝珠形盖钮，以仰莲瓣相托，下层莲瓣镂孔，便于烟香溢出；炉身为直口，平折沿，方唇，深腹，平底。腹壁饰流云纹，并铆接五只独角天龙兽足。足为浇涛，足爪四趾，以销钉套接绶带盘结的朵带环于两足之间的腹壁外。炉底有同心圆旋痕。通高 295 毫米，盖径 259 毫米，腹深 70 毫米。炉重 5363 克。

15、鎏金壸门座鸿雁纹五环银熏炉

钣金成型，纹饰涂金。由炉盘，炉座焊接而成。炉盘敞口，平折沿，斜腹壁，平底。腹壁分为五瓣，每瓣瓣心铆接一兽面铺首，口衔环耳，下套一小圆环。瓣间饰忍冬纹，炉座呈覆盆形，小直口，圆肩，宽平足沿。肩部有一周覆莲瓣，腹壁有五个镂空壸门，门中有一朵如意云头花蕾。壸门间各錾一只引颈翱翔的鸿雁、衬以蔓草，鱼子纹底。足沿錾一周莲瓣纹，内饰蔓草。通高 151 毫米，口径 195 毫米，腹深 56 毫米，底径 160 毫米，炉座高 90 毫米，足沿外径 268 毫米。重 1300 克。

16、壸门高圈足座银风炉

钣金成型，通体素净，由盖与身组成。盖沿为三层渐收的棱台，盖面呈半球形，上半部镂空，模冲出两层莲瓣，盖顶以三层银片做成的仰莲瓣承托镂空的锥顶状莲蕾。炉身为敛口，深腹，平底，圈足。口沿亦为三层渐收的棱台，每层棱台的外缘六曲。腹部上小底大，腹壁为内外两层铆合在一起。内层分作六块，与炉底铆接，外层即圈足。其腹部以下镂空六个壸门，底部与平折的足沿套接。炉底除与腹壁铆接外，其下焊有用作承

托的十字形铜片。炉身两侧的口沿下各铆接一个提耳。炉身上铆钉顶端均饰以小银花。出土时炉盖贴有墨书"大银熏炉，臣杨复恭"的签封。通高 560 毫米，盖高 313 毫米，口径 177 毫米，炉身高 252 毫米，口径 207 毫米，腹深 165 毫米，圈足外径 358 毫米。重 3920 克。

17、鎏金双蜂团花纹镂孔银香囊(大)

香囊为镂空球体，上下半球体以合页铰链相连，钩状司前控制香囊之开合。下半球体内有以两个同心圆组成的持平环，铆接香盂于其中并与球体相连。球冠有圆钮，上接 U 形银链，链端套有环勾，链下端有莲蕾饰物。上下球体均饰五朵双蜂纹团花，冠饰四蜂纹团花。球底饰折枝团花。通体为镂孔的阔叶纹样。径 128 毫米，链长 245 毫米，重 547 克。

鎏金鸿雁纹镂孔银香囊(小)

钣金成型，纹饰部分涂金。通体呈圆球状，上半球体为盖，下半球体为身，以铰链相连，子母口扣合。通体镂孔，纹饰上下对称。半球面上散点分布三个圆形规范，錾有四只鸿雁，球冠有弧形等边三角形，有内切圆于其中，圆内镂空成阔叶纹。盖顶铆接环钮，上套莲蕾形环节，其上再套置 U 形长链。勾状司前控制上下球体之开合。香囊内之香盂铆接于双层持平环上，环又与下半球体铆接，使香盂盂面始终保持平衡状态。香囊直径 58.5 毫米，持平环径分别为 38 毫米、48 毫米，香盂径 28 毫米，腹深 10 毫米。链长 177 毫米，总重 87 克。

18、鎏金仙人驾鹤纹壶门座茶罗子

器形为长方体，由盖、罗、屉、罗架、器座组成。均为钣金成型，纹饰涂金。盝顶盖面錾两体首尾相对的飞天，头顶及身侧衬以流云。盖刹四侧各饰一和合云，两侧还饰如意云头，刹边饰莲瓣纹，盖立沿饰流云纹。罗架两侧饰头束髻，着褒衣的执幡架鹤仙人，另两侧錾相对飞翔的仙鹤，四周饰莲瓣纹。罗、屉均作匣形。罗分内外两层，中夹罗网。屉面饰流云纹，有环状拉手。罗架下焊台形器座，有镂空的桃形壶门。高 95 毫米，罗身长 134 毫米，宽 84 毫米，屉长 127 毫米，宽 75 毫米，高 20 毫米，座长 149 毫米，宽 89 毫米，高 20 毫米。重 1472 克。

19、鎏金壶门座茶碾子

浇铸、钣金成型，纹饰涂金。通体为长方形，由碾槽、辖板、槽座组成。槽呈半月形尖底，口沿平折，与槽座焊接，槽口可插置辖板，辖板呈长方形。槽身两端为如意云头状，辖板中间焊接小宝珠形提手。槽身两侧各饰一只鸿雁及流云纹。槽座截面呈"Ⅱ"形，碾槽嵌于其中。槽座两端亦作如意云头。座壁有镂空壶门，门间饰天马流云纹。通高 71 毫米，长 274 毫米，槽深 34 毫米，辖板长 207 毫米，宽 30 毫米。重 1168 克。

20、纯银锅轴

轴为浇铸成型，不辐而轴，轴刃有平行沟槽，轴杆圆形，唯中部粗壮而执手之两端稍细。轴孔四周錾团花，外饰流云纹，錾文曰："轴重一十三两"。轴长 216 毫米，轴径 89 毫米。

21、摩羯纹蕾钮三足盐台

由盖、台盘、三足架等组成。盖上有莲蕾捉手，中空，有铰链可开合，与银筋焊接并与盖相连。盖心饰团花一朵，盖面饰摩羯四尾，盖沿为卷荷。三足支架与台盘焊接相连，支架以银筋盘屈而成，架中部斜出四枝，枝端有摩羯铸件二，智慧珠二。珠下且有莲蓬座，珠周有火焰纹，座下衬以团花。通高 250 毫米。

22、鎏金镂空鸿雁球路纹银笼子

模冲成型，通体镂空，纹饰鎏金。带盖，直口，深腹，平底，四足，有提梁。盖为穹顶，口沿下折与笼体扣合。顶面模冲出十五只飞鸿，内圈飞鸿引颈内向，外圈飞鸿则两两相对。口沿上缘饰一周莲瓣纹，下缘饰一周破式团花，鱼子纹底。笼体腹壁錾三周飞鸿，共二十四只，均相对翱翔。两侧口沿下铆有环耳，耳座为四瓣小团花，环耳上套置提梁，其上套有银链，另一端与盖顶相连。足呈"品"字形组合的花瓣，与笼底边缘铆接。

镂孔均作球路纹。通高 178 毫米，足高 24 毫米，重 654 克。

23、鎏金飞鸿纹银匙

匙面呈卵圆形，微凹。匙柄扁长，上宽下窄，柄端作三角形，上下部位錾花鎏金。上段为流云飞鸿，下段以联珠组成菱形图案，其间錾十字花。均以弦纹和破式菱形纹为栏界。柄背光素，长 192 毫米，匙纵径 45 毫米，横径 26 毫米，柄上端宽 13 毫米，下端宽 7 毫米。

24、系链银火筋

圆柱体，上粗下细，通体光素。顶端呈宝珠形，其下有 5 毫米宽的凹槽，环鼻套嵌其中，且与另一筋相连，链为银丝编成。筋长 276 毫米，上端径 6 毫米，下端径 2.5 毫米，链长 103 毫米。总重 765 克。

25. 捧真身菩萨

专为供奉佛指舍利而制。高髻、头戴花蔓冠。上身袒露，斜被披帛，臂饰钏，双手捧上置錾刻发愿文的镀金银匜的荷叶形盘。下着羊肠大裙，双腿左屈右跪于莲花台上。通身装饰珍珠璎珞。花蔓冠边缘串饰珍珠，冠中有坐佛；金匜呈长方形，有匜栏，长 112 毫米，宽 84 毫米。栏上贴饰 16 朵宝相花。衬以蔓草，内饰联珠纹一周。匜上錾文十一行六十五字："奉为睿文英武明德至仁大圣广孝皇帝，敬造捧真身菩萨永为供养。伏愿圣寿万春，圣枝万叶，八荒来服，四海无波。咸通十二年辛卯岁十一月十四日皇帝诞庆日记。"金匜两侧以销钉套环与护板相连。护板，长方形，长 66 毫米，宽 35 毫米。边沿饰一周几何纹样的草叶，内外缘各饰联珠一周。护板中镂空成三钴金刚杵，四周衬以缠枝蔓草。莲座呈钵形，顶面八曲，边饰联珠，顶面与底面均錾梵文，腹壁由上至下饰四层仰莲瓣，每层八瓣。上两层莲瓣内各有一尊有首光或背光，手执莲，捧琴或结跏跌坐的菩萨或声闻伎乐，两侧衬以缠枝蔓草。鼓形束腰，顶面与莲台焊接，底部以覆莲座套接。腹壁一周分别錾执剑，执斧，执塔，柱剑的四天王，余白錾三钴金刚杵。覆莲座呈覆钵形双层。外层上部一周饰八瓣覆莲，每瓣内各錾一梵文；中部一周錾八尊三头六臂金刚，均有背光。座下有立沿，饰联珠纹与莲瓣纹一周。内层中心錾十字三钴金刚杵，两侧各有一行龙，并衬以流云纹。通高 385 毫米，菩萨高 210 毫米。重 1926 克。

26、鎏金菩萨

高髻，花蔓冠，宝缯垂肩，上身袒露，左肩至右肋斜被披帛，颈饰璎珞，臂饰钏，腕戴镯。双肘平举，双手施印。下着羊肠大裙，结跏跌坐于仰莲座上，火焰纹身光。座饰每层八瓣的双层仰莲瓣，其下用销钉穿接圆形束腰，束腰下为饰八瓣覆莲的座基。通高 150 毫米，座高 45 毫米。重 651 克。

27、纯金单轮十二环锡杖

通体用纯金制成。杖杆为圆形，顶部有桃形轮杖首。轮心之杖端，为结伽跌坐于莲座上的坐佛，有背光。杖樽为宝珠形，轮顶为仰莲座智慧珠，轮侧各套有直径 22 毫米，厚 2 毫米的六枚锡环。通长 276 毫米，杖杆长 250 毫米，最大直径 6 毫米。总重 211 克。

28、鎏金单轮六环铜锡杖

锡杖由轮首、执手、杖樽三部分组成，原与木杖套接，木杖已朽坏，总长度不明。桃形轮杖首之两侧套三枚锡环，直径 117 毫米。桃形轮及圆环剖面均呈菱形。轮顶饰智慧珠。执手为八棱形，杖末为圆球形。轮高 310 毫米，宽 270 毫米，执手长 317 毫米，直径 22 毫米，杖樽长 312 毫米。

29、银金花双轮十二环锡杖

高 1960 毫米，由五十八两白银二两黄金雕铸而成。杖首有垂直相交银丝盘屈的两个桃形外轮。轮顶为仰莲束腰座，上托智慧珠一颗。外轮每面各套雕花金环三枚，共十二枚。外轮中心的杖顶又有忍冬花，流云纹，仰莲瓣组成的三重佛座，其上承托五钴杆与宝珠。杖身中空，錾刻有手持法铃，身披袈裟于莲台之上的沙弥僧十二体。锡杖通体涂刻金花，杖首刻四出团花，衬忍冬花。杖身中段刻六出团花，衬缠枝蔓草鱼子纹，间以蜀葵。下段刻一整二破二方连续团花，衬五月流云纹，整体造形装饰、雍荣华贵、制作精绝，比现藏于日本正仓院的白铜头锡杖等级高，形制宏伟得多。

30、素面云头银如意
如意柄上扁下圆，通体光素。头部为如意状。全长 600 毫米，云头宽 210 毫米。总重 405.7 克。

31、鎏金三钴杵纹臂钏
钏面鼓隆，内壁平直，钏面饰三钴金刚杵六枚，底衬蔓草，鱼子纹底。内径 92 毫米，外径 110 毫米。重 128 克—146 克。

32、迎真身纯金钵盂
圆唇，斜腹下收，小平底，通体光素。从錾文中得知，金钵是奉敕造于咸通十四年三月廿三日的。高 72 毫米，口径 212 毫米，壁厚 1.2 毫米。总重 573 克。

33、鎏金团花银钵盂
圆唇直口、鼓腹、圆底。钵外中心有阔叶团花一朵，四周散点分布扁团花五朵，花纹涂金。口缘还装饰莲瓣一周。高 73 毫米，径 79 毫米，腹深 29 毫米。总重 82 克。

34、银芙蕖
以银筋为茎、座，以银箔为花叶。主茎顶端有以莲蓬为蕊的芙蕖一朵，内外三层，共十六瓣。主茎中部分出三支茎，其一为莲蕾，其余为翻卷的荷叶。通高 410 毫米，重 535 克。

35、素面银灯
由灯盏、灯台组成。盏呈钵形，小平折沿，弧壁，深腹，圆底。口沿上立有四棱攒尖的捉手。灯台上部为盏托，下有圈足。盏托形制与灯盏相同，无口沿，盏即置于其内。圈足为喇叭形，中有棱台，足为立沿。外壁抛光，通体光素。通高 203 毫米，口径 160 毫米，盏深 63 毫米，足高 97 毫米，足径 120 毫米，壁厚 1.5 毫米。

36、盘圆座葵口小银碟
五曲葵口，平底，浅腹。碟座以银筋盘屈成螺旋形圆座。高 58 毫米，径 87 毫米。重 82 克。

37、素面银香案
钣金焊接成形，通体光素。案面平正，两端上卷。案足以银板弯曲而成，出圆肩，双足内收，双足内以银条两条焊接而成 。高 106 毫米，宽 94 毫米，案面长 155 毫米，重 605.5 克。

38、鎏金仰莲瓣荷叶圈足银碗
模冲成形，纹饰鎏金。敞口，腹壁斜收，平底，卷荷叶形圈足。碗壁模冲为两层莲瓣，错置排列，瓣尖形成口沿。圈足为翻卷荷叶，外錾叶脉。圈足底錾文："衙内都虞候兼押衙监察御史安淑布施，永为供奉。"内足壁墨书"吼"，系密教咒语，通高 80 毫米，口径 160 毫米，足径 112 毫米。重 223 克。

39、鎏金三钴杵纹银阏伽瓶
盘口，细颈，有短流，圆腹，喇叭形圈足，肩颈下饰如意云纹一周。腹部饰四个以简化莲瓣纹圈成的圆形规范，内錾十字三钴金刚杵纹，圆形规范间以两条平行线相连。腹下部有仰莲瓣一周，瓣尖之间亦饰三钴金刚杵纹，圈足饰覆莲瓣，莲瓣尖隙錾三钴金刚杵。圈足底缘饰二方连续水波纹一周。高 210 毫米，腹径 132 毫米，流长 71 毫米，底径 108 毫米。重 659.5 克。

40、双凤纹鎏金银棺
钣金成形，纹饰鎏金。棺盖为半弧形，前部錾饰莲台形华盖，其下有花结形绶带；中部以模列如意云头为栏界，其内錾饰双凤衔绶带；棺盖内壁两端有凸棱台，刚好与棺体扣合；棺体前档宽高，錾一双扇门，门扇錾饰锁和三排金钉；门上部有梯形楣额，下部饰以流云，两侧各侍立一脚踏莲花的菩萨；棺体两侧的前部各侍一金刚力士，后档则錾两只蹲狮；棺座与棺体焊接，中空，四壁均錾火焰形门。通高72毫米，棺盖长102毫米，宽45.9毫米(最宽处)，棺长82毫米，宽38毫米——48毫米，座高16.5毫米，长97毫米、宽50毫米——65毫米。重248.5克。

41、七重宝函

为供奉第一枚佛指舍利之八重宝函部分。最外层为镌刻有阿弥陀佛极乐世界等图象的檀香木盝顶宝函，出土时已残毁。第二重即鎏金四天王盝顶银宝函，第三重为素面盝顶银宝函，第四重为鎏金如来说法盝顶银宝函，第五重为六臂观音纯金宝函，第六重为金筐宝钿珍珠装纯金宝函，第七重为金筐宝钿珍珠装瑸玞石宝函，第八重为宝珠顶单檐纯金四门塔。八重宝函放置在地宫后室北壁正中部位，是整个地宫中最重要的供奉物。

42、鎏金四天王盝顶银宝函

八重宝函第二重，钣金成形，纹饰鎏金。宝函作正方体，前有司前，后有两个绞链与函盖相连；盖为盝顶，顶面錾行龙两条，四周衬以流云，每侧斜刹均錾双龙戏珠，底衬卷草；立沿各錾两体伽陵频迦鸟，鸟侧衬以海石榴与蔓草。函体四壁饰四天王像：北方大圣毗沙门天王，左手托塔，右手举剑；东方提头赖吒天王，双手持剑；西方毗娄勒叉天王，左手持弓，右手执箭；南方毗娄博叉天王，左手柱剑。身侧均侍立神将、夜叉多人。函高235毫米，边长202毫米。重699克。

43、素面盝顶银宝函

钣金成形，外壁抛光。盒体方正，盖作盝顶。盖与身以铰链相连，司前原有锁匙，以备开合，通体素净，宝函外原有绛黄色绫带封系。通高193毫米，口径长宽175毫米，函体长宽184毫米，盝顶面长宽132.5毫米。重1999克。

44、鎏金如来说法盝顶宝函

盝顶，盖与函身以铰链相连，司前贯有锁钥，钣金成形，纹饰涂金。盝顶盖面上饰四只伽陵频迦鸟，中有十字三钴金刚杵，四角亦饰三钴杵，底衬蔓草；盝刹每边有凤鸟两只，立沿每面錾两飞天，并在周围錾卧云纹。宝函正面中部为如来，四周有两菩萨，四弟子，二金刚力士，二供奉童子。佛首之侧还有捧盘飞天两体。函左为普贤菩萨，象座。周围有16名小鬼，接引使者、金刚、沙弥。菩萨上部有徐徐散落的天花。函右为文殊菩萨，狮座。小鬼、接引使者、天王、沙弥等共19名。函后有戴帷帽的坐佛。佛前有供案，上置供物三品，佛周围有四尊菩萨、二弟子、二童子。佛首之上有华盖、身后有菩提树。高162毫米，口径148毫米，底径158毫米×156毫米、盖104毫米、重1666克。

45、六臂观音纯金宝函

钣金成形，纹饰錾刻。盝顶，盖与身以铰链相连，子母口扣合。盖面錾相向翱翔之双凤，四隅饰西番莲，以单相莲瓣为规范。盝刹每面饰鸳鸯，其边栏为柳叶纹样。盖之立沿刻引颈向天飞翔的四只鸿雁，并衬以蔓草。宝函正面中部錾六臂观音坐于莲座之上，四周有六位胁侍，二童子，前置绑有案裙的香案。观音身后有四株菩提树。其余三面为坐佛，佛头设天盖，佛前设香案，案皆有案裙。高135毫米，口径129毫米，底径135毫米，盖顶84毫米，重973克。

46、金筐宝钿珍珠装瑸玞石盝顶宝函

盝顶，前后有司前及铰链。函顶四边及函体四棱均粘贴有珍珠。函体每面中心有金筐为边缘的宝相团花一朵。团花以宝石粘贴函装而成。每朵花两层，内层为四瓣松绿石，外层为八瓣红宝石。盖立沿每面有金筐鸳鸯一对。高102毫米，边长73毫米，重1022.5克。

47、宝珠顶单檐纯金四门塔

铸造成形，纯金质地。由塔身、塔座和垫片三部分组成。塔身正方，宝珠塔尖，单檐，四角起翘。宝珠饰火焰纹，其下有两层仰莲座，檐柱上錾卷草纹。塔有四门，门周有鱼子纹，门角处饰背分式流云纹。阑额及檐下均錾菱形纹饰。门下部有象征性的踏步。踏座中心焊接有高 28 毫米，直径 7 毫米的银柱，其上套置佛指舍利一枚。座面饰阔叶海石榴，座侧饰莲瓣纹一周。高 71 毫米，檐边长 48 毫米，塔座长宽 48 毫米、垫板长宽 54 毫米。重 184 克。

48、宝珠顶单檐纯金四门塔内供养的佛指舍利

此枚佛指舍利系第一枚。佛指舍利上齐下折、高下不等，三面俱平，一面稍高，色白如玉少青，质密而泽，髓穴方大，中有隐迹，二角有纹，纹并不彻。高 40.3 毫米，上宽 17.55 毫米，下宽 20.11 毫米，上内径 13.75 毫米，下内径 16.5 毫米。重 16.2 克。

49、刻花蓝琉璃盘

吹塑成形，纹饰镌刻。侈口，平沿，浅腹，平底，因使用铁捧技术整修盘缘，而盘心凸出一圆包。盘内底为一适合图案。中心为十字形花，四出部分为尖瓣，瓣心刻一"枫叶"，并以 6 字规范围于其外，中心为方格纹。方格中间隔划出斜平行线。十字花之四外角，均刻类似一字形"忍冬"花。高 23 毫米，径 200 毫米。

50、描金刻花蓝琉璃盘

侈口，翻沿，浅腹，平底，底心内凹。盘心在两周弦纹内饰蕉叶团花纹，其外为一周水波纹，波纹内刻浪花，弦纹与水波纹均为描金，中心团花刻平行的辐射线。高 23 毫米，径 157 毫米。

51、贴花盘口琉璃瓶

盘口、细颈、鼓腹、圈足。颈下有凸棱一周。腹部纹饰为四重结构；第一层为八枚黑色琉璃饼，饼心凸出一小乳钉；第二层在瓶腹中心部位，以拉丝手法将淡黄色琉璃拉成多角形饰件，粘贴瓶壁；第三层有淡黄琉璃乳钉饼六枚；第四层与第一层相同，只是将黑色琉璃饼饼沿向上又拉出个尾巴，然后粘贴于瓶壁上。圈足正中有铁捧痕迹。高 210 毫米，腹径 160 毫米。

52、葵口圈足秘色瓷碗

侈口、圆唇，腹壁斜收，五瓣碗壁、高圈足，通体涂釉，釉为淡豆绿色，晶莹细润，造型大方。高 95 毫米，径 218 毫米。

53、八棱净水瓶

小口、圆唇，长细颈，八棱瓶身，圈足。颈下有三条平行凸棱，淡豆绿色釉涂于全器。高 21 毫米，径 102 毫米。

54、琥珀狻猊

狮子类，日走五百里，食虎豹，共出土两枚，雕刻而成，表面光亮。其一半蹲卧，左前足挠首，躯体分明，色较重。通高 32 毫米，长 42 毫米。重 10.5 克；另一枚奔突状，身躯前倾，色淡。通高 20 毫米，长 43 毫米，重 5.5 克。

55、水晶枕

以水晶琢磨而成，枕面稍凹，枕侧斜收向下，小平底，与今日民间石枕无异，高 98 毫米，长 120 毫米，宽 68 毫米。

56、随球

以水晶琢磨而成，大球透明光洁，小球稍受腐蚀。"和氏之璧、随侯之球"在古代视为瑰宝。但史书多指随球为烧造的琉璃球，地宫物账明载的随球却为水晶质，可能唐代将天然宝石类亦称"随侯之球"了。大径 52 毫米，小径 40 毫米。

57、汉白玉浮雕彩绘阿育王塔

由塔刹、塔盖、塔身、塔座四部分组成。塔刹为铜铸的胡芦状，按置于盖心。塔盖为九层棱台，由上而下逐渐变大，每边刻如意云头二方连续图案一周，枭混为三棱台，由外向里收缩；塔身为四面，四角有立柱。每面中心设门，门有四排乳钉，每排六枚。门设司前，有锁。门扉两侧各有菩萨一尊，共计守护佛的舍利有八名胁侍；塔座为须弥座，每面束腰出金刚力士面首三，共计十二力士，座之棱台边沿均刻流云纹。从雕刻手法看，此塔属盛唐时期建造，而在咸通年间入藏佛指舍利时重新妆绘，三出团花即其时代特征。高 7850 毫米。

58、莲花藻井

原置于地宫后室顶部。藻井为一方石上刻出天龙衔环，大龙四周为水波，联珠。环下以银簪系结双层覆莲瓣，莲瓣为银箔镂刻而成，涂金。藻井心为两面铜镜。其中一面为鎏金背，极为少见。径 395 毫米。

59、石刻南方天王

名毗娄博叉天王，汉白玉圆石雕，头戴花冠、身着两档甲胄，而目丰满、双唇微合、双目直视远方。右手持剑，左手压在大腿之上，左腿平盘，右腿下垂，通体用红、绿、黑三色装彩、威严庄重，肃穆典雅。通高 565 毫米。

60、石刻东方天王

名提头赖吒天王，汉白玉圆雕，头戴花冠，身着两档甲胄，双唇紧闭，双手柱剑，右腿平盘、左腿下垂，通体施红、绿、黑、三彩。通高 565 毫米。

61、彩绘金毛双狮

汉白玉圆石雕，后蹲姿态，阔口大张，鬃毛卷曲、铜铃巨目虎视耽耽直视远方，通体施黄、绿、黑三彩、置于前室阿育王塔两侧，通高 593 毫米。

Explanatory Notes

Explanatory Notes:

1.Silver Tub with Gilded Patterns of Posy and Mandarin Ducks.

The tub is cast in silver , decorated with gilded designs on its surface. It has a large, sunflower-shaped mouth and a short ring foot. Around the mouth are carved the designs of lotus flower petals. The wall of the tub is shaped like four petals, on each of which are carved the pomegranate flowers and broad leaves. Two mandarin ducks spreading their wings stand face to face on lotus seats and are set off by the patterns of flowing clouds and broad leaves. Both inside and outside of the wall have the same pattern . On the bottom of the tub is a relief of a pair of mandarin ducks playing amid the pomegranate flowers and broad leaves. Either side of the tub is riveted with a piece of silver in the shape of dragon's head with the character "王"(King)on the forehead. Each dragon's mouth carries a small ring carved with a crabapple flower design and linked with a handle. Twenty-four lotus flowers are designed on the ring foot, and two characters "浙西" are engraved on the outside of the bottom .

The mouth is 460 mm in diameter; the diameter of the ring foot is 285 mm and its height is 25 mm; the wall is 6 mm in thickness, and the whole set is 145 mm in height and 6,265 g in weight.

2.Silver Box with Gilded Double-Phoenix Design Presented by Emperor.

This flat silver box has a ring foot. The lid bears a design of a pair of phoenixes both holding a ribbon from their bills in the middle and a lotus-petal design around the edge. There is also an ink inscription on the lid denoting it was presented by the emperor.

The ring foot is 17 mm in height and 180 mm in diameter. The whole piece is 95 mm in height, 215 mm in length on each side and 1,585 g in weight.

3. Gilded Silver Box in Turtle's Shape.

The silver box takes the shape of a turtle, whose head turns up and tail curls. It shrinks its feet under the hard shell; the body is hollowed in oval form. The turtle's head is joined with the body, which in turn joins the tail. The patterns on all parts very much resemble those on a real turtle, and therefore it looks life-like.

The turtle is 130 mm in height, 280 mm in length and 150 mm in width.

4.Curve-Rimmed Silver Box with Gilded Double-Lion Pattern and Ring Foot.

The box has a lid with a broad curve rim, a body with a broad curve rim and a flat bottom, and a ring foot. The top of the lid has a decoration of two leaping lions set off by broad leaves and entwining vine and framed by two lozenges (one inside, the other outside) formed by two strings of pearls. The two rims bear the same pattern of broad leaves and entwining vine. The ring foot has the pattern of lotus petals.

The mouth of the body is 173 mm × 168 mm . The ring foot is 24 mm in height, 148 mm in length and 138 mm in width. The whole set is 120 mm in height and 799 g in weight.

5. Oblong Silver Box with Plain Surface.

The box is well polished without any decorative designs.The lid has corrugations along the edge and a spread brim 3mm wide. The walls of the box are upright, the bottom flat and the ring foot short.

It is 97 mm in height, 173 mm in length, 119 mm in width, and 605.5 g in weight.

6.Silver Box with Plain Surface and Ring Foot.

This silver box has a lid, a body with upright walls and a flat bottom, and a ring foot. Both the inside and outside of the lid bear traces of being turned by the lathe. A hole is seen at the very center of the lid. The whole box is well polished, free of any decorative pattern.

The ring foot is 21 mm in height and 152 mm in diameter. The whole box is 816.5 g in weight.

7. Silver Box in the Shape of Chinese Crabapple Flower with Double—Swan—Goose Pattern..

The box takes the shape of the flower of the Chinese crabapple. The decorations are died out. The lid is convex, with the pattern of a pair of swan—geese in symmetry spreading their wings and ready to fly. It is 20 mm in height, 51 mm in length, 36 mm in width and 20 g in weight.

8.Copper Box Carved with Pattern of Four Tridents.

The box is died into shape and carved with designs. On the lid is a pattern of four fridents. All the surface has become rusty.

The box is 51 mm in height, 104 mm in diameter, and 196.5 g in weight. .

9.Gilded Boxes with Hollowed—Out Ring Foot.

The whole set consists of five pieces, all of the same type, one set upon another. Each has a short upright body and a flat bottom. Only the outside of the body is gilded. To the inside of the bottom is soldered a grill in the form of a cross. It has a ring foot and the ring has six hollowed—out holes. In between there are designs of honeysuckle. On the outside of the bottom are found traces of concentric circles.

The height of each layer is 38.7 mm, the diameter of the mouth is 102.8 mm; the outer diameter of the foot is 112 mm, and the depth of the body is 11.9 mm .The weight of each piece is 243 g while that of the total is 1,235 g.

10. Gilded Silver Jar with Human Images.

Decorated with gilded patterns, the jar has a lid, an upright deep body with a flat bottom and a ring foot. The knob of the lid takes the shape of a pearl, and the lid is designed in the form of four petals, each bearing a died—out flying lion, whose detail section is finished by engraving .The lion is set off by entwining vine. All borders of the petals are decorated with S—shaped designs. The lid is joined to the body by a snap fastener. The wall of the jar has four gate patterns carved respectively with such human and animal images as two fairies playing the Chinese chess, Yu Boya(a legendary musician) playing the Chinese harp, Xiao Shi(another legendary musician) playing the flute and a golden snake sending forth from its mouth a pearl.

The jar is 247 mm in height, 132 mm in diameter and 883.5 g. in weight. The body is 112 mm deep and the ring foot is 126 mm across.

11.Gilded Cup with Images of Musicians.

With patterns gold—coated, this cup has a domed lid, an upright deep body with a flat bottom and a ring foot. The lid is carved with the pattern of a circle of entwining vine. The edge of the lid is carved with patterns of water waves and lotus petals. At the top is a pearl—shaped knob, set off by a circle of lotus petals, two mandarin ducks and a flying bird surrounded by entwining vine. The body of the cup has a waist and the brim of the mouth is decorated with entwining vine. Around the waist are carved images of musicians and dancers set off again by entwining vine. The lower part of the body is encircled by a lotus−petal pattern. The foot takes the shape of a bell with a hoop over its top while the edge of the bell is carved with lotus leaves.

The whole piece is 117 mm in height and 149.5 g in weight. The diameter of the lid is 56 mm, that of the mouth 54 mm and that of the foot 63 mm, while the height of the body is 58 mm.

12.Gilded Silver Bowl with Lotus−Leaf−Shaped Ring Foot.

The silver bowl, cast into the shape, consists of three parts: the bowl, the lid and the ring foot. The domed lid has a knob in the form of a lotus bud, around which are carved the patterns of seven petals of plum blossom and four sets of openwork moving clouds. The bowl has a plain surface, a spread mouth, a curved wall and a round bottom. The ring foot is welded to the bottom of the bowl and formed in the lotus−leaf shape .

The whole set is 98 mm in height, 213.5 g in weight; the lid is 45 mm in height and 71 mm in diameter; the mouth of the bowl is 66.5 mm in diameter; the depth is 24 mm ; the ring foot is 27 mm in height and 80 mm in diameter.

13.Silver Dish with Gilded Posy Design.

The silver dish, died into the shape, bears gilded designs on the surface. There are altogether twenty pieces of its kind, with or without a ring foot. The edge of the dish is shaped in the form of five sunflower petals. In the center of each petal is a cross−shaped flower pattern. In the center of the bottom is a posy with broad leaves.

The footless dish is 120 g in weight, 14 mm in height and 102 mm in diameter; the footed dish is 19 mm in height, 130 g in weight, 102 mm in diameter.

14. Five−Footed Silver Incense Burner with Gilded Lotus−Petal Designs and Turtle Decorations.

The burner's domed lid bears a honeysuckle design on its broad spread brim, a lotus−petal design on the dome's edge and five lotus flowers on the dome's surface. Upon each of the flowers lies a turtle with its head turning around and its mouth gripping herbs. The knob is supported by three layers of lotus petals, with the bottom layer hollowed out to let the fragrant smoke of the incense spread out. The burner's body has a deep belly, a spread brim and a flat bottom. The wall is engraved with a moving −cloud design and riveted with five feet made in the shape of a unicorn's head and leg. Between the feet hang totally five decorative pendants in the shape of a ribbon−woven badge.

The lid is 259 mm in diameter. The body is 70 mm in height . The whole burner is 295 mm in height and 5,363 g in weight.

15.Silver Incense Burner with Gilded Swan−Goose Patterns and Hollowed−Out Seat.

The body of the burner takes the shape of an upside−down bell with a large spread mouth and a small flat bottom. The wall is made in the form of five petals. Each petal is riveted in the center with a metal beast head gripping in its mouth a metal ring linked with another ring. These decorations are set off by honeysuckle designs. The burner's seat is shaped like an upside−down basin with a spread mouth. The seat wall's upper part is encircled by a lotus−petal pattern. The middle part is hollowed out in the design of five gates with a cloud−shaped bud set in each of them. There is an engraved soaring swan—goose surrounded by an entwining vine and fishroe pattern between every two gates. The lower edge of the seat is decorated with a circle of a lotus—petal and entwining vine pattern.

The body's mouth is 195 mm in diameter；its bottom，160 mm in diameter；its height is 56 mm. The seat is 90 mm in height；its ring—foot's outer diameter is 268 mm. The whole set is 151 mm in height and 1,300 g in weight.

Made up of the lid and the body，this burner is unique in its complete plainness. The lid takes the shape of a dome with the brim bearing a three—layer corrugation gradually drawing in. The upper half of the lid is hollowed into two layers of lotus petals. The knob of the lid is made of three silver plates and shaped into a hollow lotus bud，supported by lotus petals. The burner has a contracted mouth，a deep body with a flat bottom and a ring foot. The brim of the body also bears a corrugation of three layers gradually drawing in. The body is larger in size at the base and smaller at the top. The wall is of two layers joined by rivets. The inner layer is divided into six parts and riveted onto the bottom，and the outer layer forms the ring foot. The lower half of the body is hollowed out into six gates . The bottom is joined to the the foot. Apart from being riveted with the wall of the body，the bottom is also supported by a copper cross，which is soldered to the bottom. From either side of the body hangs a handle. All the rivets on the body are decorated with small silver flowers. When it was unearthed there was a handwritten sealing label stuck to the lid which reads: "The Large Silver Incense Burner" together with the sealer's name.

The burner is 560 mm in height and 3，920 g in weight. Height of the lid is 313 mm，with a diameter of 177 mm，The body is 252 mm tall，and the diameter of the mouth 207 mm. Depth of the body is 165 mm. The outer diameter of the foot is 358 mm.

17.A.Openwork Silver Censer with Gilded Double—Bee and Posy Design. (Large)
B. Openwork Silver Censer with Gilded Swan—Goose Design. (Small)

A.Openwork Silver Censer with Gilded Double—Bee and Posy Design.(Large)

The censer，ball—shaped，consists of two halves. The upper half is the lid and the lower half，the body. Both halves are punched into an openwork pattern of broad leaves，hinged together and closed by a hook. The upper half has a ring—knob linked with a silver chain，a four—bee and posy design on the top under the ring—knob，and five double—bee and posy designs around the lower surface. The lower half also bears five double—bee and posy designs symmetrical to those on the upper，but it has a design of floral sprays on the bottom. Inside is an incense—burning basin that has a special gyroscopic mechanism which allows the basin to stay upright all the time whatever way the censer is turned.

Diameter: 128 mm；weight: 547 g；chain length: 245 mm.

B. Openwork Silver Censer with Gilded Swan—Goose Design. (Small)

The censer，ball—shaped. consists of two halves. The upper half is the lid and the lower half，the body. Both halves are punched into an openwork pattern，hinged together and closed by a snap fastener. The upper half has a ring—knob linked with a silver chain. On the top under the knob is a curve—side equilateral triangle with an inscribed circle, which is hollowed into a broad-leaf pattern. On the lower surface spread three circles and four swan geese. The lower half bears the same patterns. Inside is an incense-burning basin that has a gyroscopic mechanism the same as that inside the large censer.

Of the gyroscopic mechanism, the outer ring is 48 mm in diameter and the inner ring, 38 mm in diameter. The incense-burning basin is 28 mm in diameter and 10 mm in height. The silver chain is 177 mm in length. The cencer is 58.5 mm in diameter and 87 g in weight.

18.Tea Sifter with Gilded Fairy-Riding-Crane Design and Hollow-Out Seat.

This set of tea processing tool consists of a lid, a sifter, a drawer and a seat. The lid has a flat top and four sides. The top is engraved with two flying apsarases surrounded by a moving-cloud design. The four sides are decorated with cloud and lotus-petal designs. The sifter is made in the shape of a box . The box bears the decoration of a fairy riding a flying crane on its two sides, and a flying-crane and lotus-petal design on the other two sides. The drawer has a knob on its front side decorated with a moving-cloud design .The box is welded with the seat, whose wall is hollowed into a number of gates.

The sifter is 134 mm in length and 84 mm in width. The drawer is 127 mm in length, 75 mm in width and 20 mm in height. The seat is 149 mm in length, 89 mm in width and 20 mm in height. The whole set is 95 mm in height and 1,472 g in weight.

19. Tea-Grinding Mortar with Hollowed-Out Seat and Gilded Designs.

This set consists of a tea-grinding mortar, a metal board and a seat. The mortar is made in the shape of a crescent, whose two curved walls narrow down to join each other at the bottom. The metal board is oblong and can be fixed to the mouth of the mortar. The board has a knob in the center of its upper side. The mortar is set in the slot of the seat . Both ends of the seat are engraved with a cloud design. Each side of the seat is hollowed into three gates. Between the gates spreads a cloud design.

The crescent-shaped mortar is 34 mm in depth. The metal board is 207 mm in length and 30 mm in width. The whole set is 71 mm in height, 274 mm in length and 1,168 g in weight.

20.Wheel-Shaped Silver Grinding Roller.

The roller takes a solid wheel's shape with an axle vertically penetrating through its center. Both the wheel-shaped roller and the axle are cast into the shape. The axle is thick in its middle part and thin at both ends, which serve as two handles. Around the center of the wheel is engraved a posy pattern set off by a circle of moving-cloud design. The roller bears an inscription saying: "This grinding roller weighs 13 taels."

The axle is 216 mm long and the wheel-shaped roller is 89 mm in diameter.

21.Salt Basin with Fish Pattern and Tripod.

This set consists of a lid , a basin and a tripod. The lid has a hollow knob in the shape of a lotus bud, The knob is hinged with the lid and set off by an engraved design of posy. The middle space of the lid is decorated with the pattern of four fishes. The lower edge of the lid bears a circle of lotus-leaf pattern. The tripod is soldered to the bottom of the basin. Its three legs are built with coiled silver wire, from the middle of which shoot out four decorative branches. Each branch's end carries two cast fishes and two pearls with a lotus seat set off by a flame design and a posy pattern.

The whole set is 250 mm high.

22.Openwork Silver Cage with Gilded Swan—Goose and Lotus Design.

The cage consists of a lid, a body, four feet and a loop handle. Both the lid and the body are punched into the openwork shape. The convex lid bears the images of 15 flying swan geese arranged in two circles on the surface, a design of lotus petals around the edge's upper space and a pattern of floral sprays and fishroe marks around the edge's lower space. The body carries 24 flying swan geese arranged in three circles. Two loop ears are riveted to both sides of the mouth. The loop handle is set to the two ears. The four feet, made in the shape of petal cluster, are riveted to the body's bottom rim.

The feet are all 24 mm in height. The whole cage is 178 mm in height and 654 g in weight.

23.Silver Spoon with Gilded Pattern of Flying Swan Goose.

The spoon has an oval and shallow bowl, a long handle and a triangular end. The face of the handle bears gilded patterns: a flying swan goose surrounded by flowing clouds on the upper, and many designs of pearl—string in the form of lozenge on the lower. There are also designs of flowers within the lozenges. The back of the handle is free of any decoration.

The whole length is 192 mm; the length of the bowl is 45 mm, and the width is 26 mm; the width for the upper part of the handle is 13 mm and for the lower, 7 mm.

24.Silver Fire—Tongs with Chain.

The tongs are made of silver , with a polished plain surface. Each piece has a pearl— shaped top.The tongs are linked by a silver chain.

Each piece is 276 mm in length ; the upper end is 6 mm in diameter and the lower 2.5 mm in diameter. The chain is 103 mm long. The whole pair weighs 765 g.

25.Bodhisattva to Carry Sakyamuni's Sarira.

The Bodhisattva is half—naked, wearing a flower—vine—designed and pearl—rimmed hat and a long skirt, and half—kneeling on a lotus seat. Held in both hands of the Bodhisattva is a leaf—shape, oblong tray containing a piece of gold plate. The gold plate carries an engraved text in 65 Chinese characters to the effect that this Bodhisattva was made on the order of the emperor in the twelfth year of Xiantong to carry Sakyamuni's sarira. The plate is 112 mm long and 84 mm wide. The bowl—shaped lotus seat is welded with a drum, which is plugged into an upsidedown—bowl—shaped lotus base. The wall of the lotus seat is decorated with the images of Bodhisattvas and musicians. The drum's wall is decorated with the images of four Devarajas. The base bears a lo-tus—petal design around its upper surface, eight images of three—head, six—arm Vajras around its lower surface, and a rim of pearl and lotus—petal design at its bottom edge.

The Bodhisattva is 210 mm high. The whole piece is 385 mm in height and 1,926 g in weight.

26. Gilded Bodhisattva.

With the upper part of the body naked , the Bodhisattva has a tall hair bun and a flower—and—vine—de-signed hat. A silk flap hangs over the shoulders. Around the neck is a string of pearls. and around the arm and wrists are an armlet and bracelets. For the lower part of the body the buddha wears a long skirt, sitting cross-legged on a lotus seat with a halo of flames in the backgound. The seat is decorated with two layers of lotus petals, and fixed to the base.

The whole piece is 150 mm in height and 651 g in weight. The height of the seat is 45 mm.

27.Gold Staff with Twelve Rings Linked in Single Wheel.

The staff is made of gold. At the top of the round shaft is fixed a peach-shape wheel. From both sides of the wheel hang free twelve small rings, equally divided in number. Each of the rings is 2 mm thick and 22 mm in diameter. Both ends of the shaft bear Buddhist decorations.

The shaft is 6 mm in diameter and 250 mm in length. The whole staff is 276 mm in length and 211 g in weight.

28.Gilded Copper Staff with Six Rings Linked in Single Wheel.

The copper staff is gilded and consists of three parts: a peach-shaped wheel, a handle and a butt . Originally, the three parts were connected with two pieces of wooden shafts , which are now rotten to ashes. The whole length is therefore unknown. In either side of the peach-shaped wheel are linked three copper rings. The diameter of each ring is 117 mm.The handle is octagonal , and the butt end is like a ball.

The height of the wheel is 310 mm, its width is 270 mm; the length of the handle is 317 mm, its diameter is 22 mm; the length of the butt is 312 mm.

29.Silver and Gold Staff with Flower Designs and Twelve Rings Linked in Two Wheels.

This monk's staff, 1,960 mm long, is cast in 58 taels of silver and 2 taels of gold. Fixed to the top of the staff's shaft are two crossed wheels made of silver strands. Linked in the two wheels are twelve gold rings carved in the flower design, divided in equal number on the wheels' four semicircles. Set on top of the shaft is a Buddhist seat made up of three layers of lotus petals and engraved with honeysuckle and moving —cloud patterns. The seat carries a pentadent and pearl decoration. The hollow shaft is carved with the images of twelve sramaneras wearing Kasaya and standing on the lotus seat. The images are set off by gold-coated floral engravings. The top section of the shaft bears four posies set off by honeysuckle. The middle section carries six posies set off by entwining vine, fishroe and hollyhock. The lower section shows chained posies set off by moving clouds.The staff is magnificent in design and exquisite in craftsmanship, by far superior to the copper— nickel —top staff kept in Japan's Shosoin treasure house.

30.Silver Ruyi (S—Shaped Ornament) with Plain Surface.

This Ruyi has a handle with a flat face and a curved back. The head takes the shape of cloud. The surface is free of any decoration.

It is 600 mm in length, and 405.7 g in weight; the head is 210 mm in width.

31.Gilded Armlet with Designs of Tridents.

The face of this armlet is curved but the back is flat. The armlet is decoraed with designs of six tridents,. set off by entwining vine and fishroe.

The inside diameter of the armlet is 92 mm and the outside 110 mm. The weight is 128—146 g .

32.Pure Gold Alms Bowl Used to Welcome Sakyamuni's Sarira.

Free of any decorations, the bowl has a round brim and a sloping wall so that the flat bottom is relatively small. The inscription on it says that it was made on the emperor's order, on the 23rd day of the third month of the 14th year of Xiantong under the Reign of Emperor Yizong.

The alms bowl is 72 mm in height, 573 g in weight; the diameter of the mouth is 212 mm, the thickness of the wall is 1.2 mm.

33.Gilded Silver Alms Bowl with Posy Designs.

This alms bowl has a round brim, a fat belly and a round bottom. At the center of the outside surface is a design of posy with broad leaves, surrounded by five oval—shaped designs of flowers.The flowers are gilded. The edge of the mouth is decorated with patterns of lotus petals.

Its height is 73 mm, the diameter 79 mm. The weight is 82 g and the depth of the body is 29 mm.

34.Silver Lotus Flower.

Supported by a silver stalk with leaves made of silver foils, this lotus flower stands erect together with a seedpod. The flower has three layers of a total of 16 petals. And from the mid—point of the stalk branch out three smaller stems. One of them carries a bud, the other two have folded leaves.

It is 410 mm in height and 535 g in weight.

35.Silver Lamp with Plain Surface.

The lamp consists of two parts: the oil cup and the stand. The cup takes the shape of a bowl with a spread brim. a curved wall, a deep body and a round bottom. To the brim of the cup is fixed a handle. The top of the stand is the holder for the cup, while the bottom is a ring foot .The holder fits the cup very well. The ring foot is in the form of a bell, the outer wall of which is well polished but without any decorations.

The whole piece is 203 mm in height. The cup is 160 mm in diameter and 63 mm in depth. The ring foot is 97 mm in height, 120 mm in diameter, and the wall is 1.5 mm thick.

36.Silver dishes.

The dish is made of silver and set on a coiled silver—wire stand. The set of dish and stand is 58 mm in height and 82 g in weight. The dish is 87 mm in diameter. Seen here are three dishes.

37.Silver Incense—Burner Table with Plain Surface.

The table is made of silver plates. Its top is oblong, with the two ends turning a little bit upward. The support consists of two silver plates connected with two silver rods at the base.

The table is 106 mm in height, 605.5 g in weight, 94 mm in width; the top is 155 mm in length.

38.Gilded Silver Bowl in the Shape of Lotus Flower with Lotus—Leaf—Shaped Ring Foot.

The silver bowl, died into shape , takes the form of a lotus flower. On the wall are carved two layers of petals. The mouth takes the form of lotus flower petals, and the ring foot, the form of the lotus leaf with veins engraved on it. On the outside of the bottom there is an inscription relating that the bowl was offered by An Shu, a royal inspector. Inside the bottom a character "吼"(a kind of incantation of Buddhism)is written.

The bowl is 80 mm high, weighing 223 g ; the diameter is 160 mm for the mouth and 112 mm for the ring foot.

39. Gilded Silver Pitcher with Patterns of Tridents.

The pitcher has a dish—like mouth, a narrow neck, a round body with a spout and a ring foot in the shape of a bell. Below the neck is a circle of cloud patterns. The surface of the body is decorated with four circular sketches of lotus petals, within each of which is carved a design of four tridents. Further down the body is a circle of lotus petals. The ring foot is carved with lotus petals. The edge of the ring foot has patterns of water waves.

The pitcher's height is 210 mm and the weight 659.5 g . The diameters of the body and the bottom are 132 mm and 108 mm respectively.

40. Gilded Silver Coffin with Double—Phoenix Pattern.

This coffin has a lid , a body and a base with gilded patterns. The lid takes the shape of a convex tile. The front of the surface of the lid is carved with a canopy in the form of a lotus seat with dangling ribbons. The middle bordered by cloud patterns, is carved with two phoenixes , carrying ribbons in their bills . The two ends of the inside surface of the coffin lid are soldered with bars which help fix tight the lid to the body of the coffin. The body has a larger front end, carved with a pattern of a double—door decorated with a padlock and three rows of gold studs. The lintel of the door is in the shape of a trapezoid and the lower part of the door is decorated with drifting clouds . Standing on both sides of the double door are two Bodhisattvas on lotus flowers. On the front parts of both sides of the body are carved vajra—warriors. On the rear end are carved two sitting lions. The body and the base of the coffin are soldered together, leaving the inside hollow. The four sides of the base are hollowed into gates with flames in the background.

The whole piece is 72 mm in height. The lid is 102 mm in length, 45.4 mm in width. The body of the coffin is 82 mm in height, 38—48 mm in width. The base is 16.5 mm in height, 97 mm in length, 50—65 mm in width. The total weight of the coffin is 248.5 g .

41. Seven Precious Caskets, One Successively Smaller than Another.

The caskets are part of the eight ones for enshrining the first finger bone of Sakyamuni. The first. or the outermost, is a sandalwood casket carved with the image of Amida Buddha and the Buddhist Paradise. The casket was already rotten when discovered. The second is a gilded silver casket with the images of four Devarajas (Heavenly Guardians). The third is a silver casket with a gilded surface without any pattern on it. The fourth is a gilded casket made of silver, with the image of Tathagata preaching Buddhism. The fifth is made of pure gold, with the image of six—armed Avalokitesvara. The sixth is also made of pure gold and inlaid with pearls. The seventh is a marble casket decorated with pearls and gems. The eighth, made of pure gold, takes the form of stupa crowned with a gem top and has four small gates in the four walls.

The eight precious caskets, placed in the center of the rear chamber in the crypt, are most important relics of Buddhist culture.

42. Gilded Silver Casket with Four Devarajas' Images.

This is No.2 of the eight caskets enshrining Sakyamuni's sarira. The casket is nearly cubic. Its lid is hinged to the body on the back side and locked to body on the front. The top surface of the lid is engraved with two dragons set off by flowing clouds; each of the four slopes is carved with two dragons scrambling for a pearl, set off by entwining vine; and each of the four vertical sides bears a bird image set off by a pomegranate and entwining vine pattern. On the four walls of the body are the images of Devarajas of the North, the South, the East and the West, carrying their weapons in the hands, supported by a number of images of generals of the Heaven and ghosts from the Hell.

The whole casket is 235 mm high and 202 mm square, and 699 g in weight.

43.Silver Casket with Plain Surface.

The casket is nearly cubic in form and well polished. The lid and the body are hinged on the back side and locked on the front. The casket has a plain surface. It was tied by a dark yellow silk ribbon when it was placed in the rear chamber of the crypt.

The casket is 193 mm in height, 184 mm in length and in width, and 1,999 g in weight; the mouth is 175 mm square; the top of the lid is 132.5 mm square.

44.Gilded Silver Casket with Image of Tathagata Preaching Buddhism.

The casket consists of a lid and a body, joined by hinges on the back side and closed by a lock on the front. The surface of the top is carved with four birds and a pattern of four tridents in the middle. The corners are also decorated with tridents set off by entwining vine. On the slopes of the lid are phoenixes. Along each vertical side are carved two flying Apsarases surrounded by clouds.On the front wall of the body is carved Tathagata flanked by two buddhas, four disciples. two vajras and two attending lads, On either side of Tathagata are two more flying Apsarases holding trays in their hands . On the left wall is carved Samantabhadra riding an elephant, surrounded by 16 servants, ushers, vajras and sramaneras. Over the head of the Bodhisattva are seen flowers. On the right wall is Manjusri riding a lion, attended by 19 servants, sramaneras, Devarajas and ushers. On the back wall is the sitting Buddha wearing a hat surrounded by 4 Bodhisattvas, 2 disciples and 2 attending lads. In front of the Budda is an altar and three kinds of offerings. Over the head of the Budda is a canopy and behind him is a bodhi tree.

The body's mouth is 148 mm square. The base is 158 mm × 156 mm. The whole casket is 162 mm in height and 1,666 g in weight.

45.Pure Gold Casket with Image of Six—Armed Avalokitesvara.

Carved with patterns, this casket consists of a lid and a body. The lid and the body are joined by hinges and fastened by a snap. The top surface of the lid are carved with two flying phoenixes facing each other .The four corners of the top are decorated with lotus flowers. The four slopes of the lid are carved with mandarin ducks edged by the pattern of willow leaves. The vertical rim of the lid has four swan geese soaring skyward, set off by entwining vine. At the very center of the casket's front wall is carved the six—armed Avalokitesvara sitting on a lotus seat, flanked by six attendants and two lads. In front of the Bodhisattva is an incense burner table covered with a table—cloth. Behind are four bodhi trees. On the remaining three walls are seated buddhas. All have an incense burner table before them.

The whole piece is 135 mm in height and 973 g in weight. The mouth is 129 mm square; the base ,135 mm square;the top surface of the lid, 84 mm square.

46.Marble Casket Decorated with Gems and Pearls.

The casket consists of a lid and a body. The four top edge of the lid and the four vertical edges of the body are decorated with pearls. In the center of each side of the body there is a decoration of gold—framed rosette, with its petals made of different gems . Each vertical side of the lid is decorated with a pair of mandarin ducks.

The casket is 102 mm ×73 mm×73 mm, 1,022.5 g in weight.

47.Pure Gold Stupa Enshrining Sakyamuni's Finger Bone.

The stupa is cast in gold. The ball—shaped gem top of the roof is set on a lotus seat. The roof has four slopes. The body, square—based, has a gate in each of its walls. The gate's frame is decorated with a design, which is flanked by moving clouds. The base bears pomegranate designs on its top level sides and lotus—petal designs on its vertical sides. Inside the stupa hides a stand with a silver rod welded to its center. The sarira(finger bone of Sakyamuni) is held by the rod.

Each side of the roof's edge is 48 mm long; that of the base's edge is 48 mm long; that of the stand's edge is 54 mm long. The whole stupa is 71 mm in height and 184 g in weight.

48. Sakyamuni's Finger Bone Enshrined in the Pure Gold Stupa.

This is the first of the four Sakyamuni's finger bones found in the crypt. It is pure and white, with short crevices on two corners.

The bone is 40.3 mm in height and 16.2 g in weight. The upper end's inner width is 13.75 mm while the outer width is 17.55 mm. The lower end's inner width is 16.5 mm while the outer width is 20.11 mm.

49.Blue Glass Dish Carved with Flower Designs.

The dish is blown into the shape, carved with designs. It has a flat bottom with a convex part in the center. On the inside surface is carved a cross—shaped pattern with four maple leaves .The four corners outside the cross pattern are carved with honeysuckles.

The dish is 23 mm in height, and 200 mm in diameter.

50. Blue Glass Dish with Patterns Traced in Gold.

This shallow dish has a flat bottom with a concave center.The central part of the bottom is a carved pattern of palm—leaves enclosed by two circles. Outside is a pattern of water waves and sprays. All the patterns are traced in gold.

The dish is 23 mm in height and 157 mm in diameter.

51.Glass Vase with Plaque Patterns and Dish—Edge Mouth.

The vase has a dish—edge mouth, a narrow neck, a fat belly and a ring foot. Below the neck is a raised line circling around. The belly is decorated with four circles of patterns. The first consists of eight round cake—shaped glass ornaments. The second has multiangular patterns made of glass. The third includes six yellowish glass nipple—shaped nails. The fourth has ornaments similar to the first. In the center of the bottom there is a mark left by iron rod when it was produced .

The vase is 210 mm in height, 160 mm in diameter .

52. Secret Porcelain Bowl with Sunflower—Shaped Mouth and Ring Foot.

This bowl has a wide flared mouth . The body contracts from the mouth to the base. The wall is made in the shape of five petals. The ring foot is fairly tall. The whole bowl is glazed in light green .The glaze is exceptionally fine and glossy， which， together with other qualities， lends the bowl unusual beauty.

Height: 95 mm; diameter: 218 mm.

53.Clean Water Jar with Fat Octagonal Belly.

The jar has a small mouth， a long neck， a fat octagonal belly and a ring foot. It is glazed in light green.

The jar is 21 mm in height; the diameter of the belly is 102 mm.

54. Amber Lions.

According to classical Chinese literature， this kind of lion (pronounced in Chinese / suanni /) can cover 250 km a day and eat the tiger and the leopard. Found in the crypt are two skillfully—sculptured， finely—polished amber lions， one in a sitting posture， one in a running posture.

The sitting one is darker in color， 32 mm in height， 42 mm in length and 10.5 g in weight. The running one is 20 mm in height， 43 mm in length and 5.5 g in weight.

55. Crystal Pillow.

This finely—polished crystal pillow looks exactly the same as the stone pillow still used by country folks in China today.

It is 98 mm in height， 120 mm in length and 68 mm in width.

56.Marquis Sui's Balls.

In ancient Chinese culture, "Mr He's jade and Marquis Sui's ball" are known as the most precious gems .But the Marquis Sui's ball as is described in classical literature is made of glass， while the two Marquis Sui's balls found in the crypt are made of crystal according to the description made in the stone list. This fact explains that the material used to make Marquis Sui's balls was widened to include crystal and other kinds of precious stones during the Tang times.

The large ball， 52 mm in diameter， still looks polished and transparent， and the small one， 40 mm in diameter， is already somewhat eroded.

57.Painted White—Marble Asoka Pagoda.

The pagoda consists of four parts: the top， the roof， the body and the base. The top is made of copper, cast into the shape of a bottle gourd and fixed to the roof. The roof is made in a nine—tier design. The body has four walls. Each wall has a gate with a lock.On both sides of the the gate there is a Bodhisattva guarding Sakyamuni's sarira preserved inside. The base bears three Vajras' faces on each of its four waist sides above its three—tier bottom. The bottom edge is engraved with the moving —cloud design.

The whole pagoda is 7,850 mm in height.

58.Vault Center Panel with Lotus Flower Designs.

Originally set at the center of the vault of the rear chamber in the crypt， this is a square stone tablet carved with a heavenly dragon carrying a ring in its mouth. Around the dragon are water waves and pearls. Below the ring are two layers of lotus petals joined together by a silver pin. The petals are carved out of silver foils and then painted with gold. To the centre of the panel are attached two brass mirrors, one of which has a gilded back. This is a true rarity.

The panel is 395 mm square.

59.Southern Devaraja(Heavenly Guardian).

The statue is carved from a round piece of white marble. It wears armour and a hat decorated with flowers. It has a round face and a half closed mouth. The right hand carries a sword, the left rests on the left leg. It is in a half sitting posture, and painted in red, green and black, looking solemn and majestic.

Height: 565 mm

60. Eastern Devaraja (Heavenly Guardian).

The image is carved out of a round piece of white marble. It wears armour and a hat decorated with flowers, with its mouth closed and hands holding a sword. The right leg is bent and the left one hangs down. It is painted in red, green and black.

Height: 565 mm.

61.Two Painted Lions with Golden Hair.

The lions are carved from white marble, in sitting posture, with wide open mouth and curled mane. Their fierce eyes stare into the distance. The two animals serve as guards on either side of the Asoka pagoda. They are painted in yellow, green and black.

Height: 593 mm.

Compiler: Shi Xingbang

Chinese Text Writer: Han Wei

（陕）新登字 003 号

法门寺地宫珍宝

法门寺考古队

石兴邦　选　编

韩　伟　图版解说

陕西 人民美术出版社 出版发行

（西安北大街 131 号）

新华书店 经销　　宝鸡市人民印刷厂印刷

787×1092 毫米　12 开本　　12 印张　　50 千字

1989 年 3 月第 1 版　　1994 年 5 月第 2 次印刷

印数：4,001—9,000

ISBN 7—5368—0647—7

J.542　定价：39.50 元

责任编辑　　邵梦龙
装帧设计

摄　　影　　王保平
　　　　　　周式中
翻　　译　　穆善培
　　　　　　徐启升

Editor and Binding Designer:　Shao Menglong
Photographer:　Wang Baoping
English Translators:　Zhou Shizhong
　　　　　　Mu Shanpei
　　　　　　Xu Qisheng